EXCEPTIONAL HOMES SINCE 1864

The Classic Style of RALF SCHMITZ

RS

EXCEPTIONAL HOMES SINCE 1864

The Classic Style of RALF SCHMITZ

Vol. **2**

RS

Architecture & Artistry

History & Vision

Design & Style

Das gute Haus:
Zur Zusammenarbeit mit RALF SCHMITZ

UNIVERSITY OF NOTRE DAME, SPÄTSOMMER 2022
Sebastian Treese, Architekt

Meine Zusammenarbeit mit RALF SCHMITZ, die vor etwa zehn Jahren begonnen hat, ist eine von Spannungen und Auseinandersetzungen, von Erfolgen und Rückschlägen geprägte Zeit. Außergewöhnlich sind die Häuser, die im Konzert wirtschaftlicher Vernunft, technischer Solidität und schöpferischer Kraft entstanden sind. Der konzertanten Aufführung verwandt, gleicht kein Haus dem anderen, kein Projekt lässt den Verdacht von Nachlässigkeit oder Müdigkeit erkennen. Im Gegenteil: Über die Jahre entstanden immer mutigere und selbstverständlichere Häuser. Im Zentrum aber steht die Wohnung, an deren Partitur in jedem Projekt gefeilt wird. Erkenntnisse aus zurückliegenden Vorhaben fließen ein, wie sich verändernde Anforderungen an das Wohnen im Zeitalter von Pandemie und politisch-gesellschaftlichem Wandel. Aus der Auseinandersetzung mit dem Ort, dem Respekt vor der Nachbarschaft und der Besinnung auf lokale Bautraditionen entstehen Häuser, deren Anspruch es ist, so gut zu sein, als würde man sie für sich selbst bauen.

2012 engagierte mich das Familienunternehmen RALF SCHMITZ zunächst als Bildkünstler, um die aktuellen Bauvorhaben zu visualisieren. „Bauen aus Leidenschaft" stand damals über der Tür – ob das denn stimme, wollte ich unbedingt wissen. Zu diesem Zeitpunkt hatte im Unternehmen die nächste Generation die Bühne betreten. Was es heißt, mit Leidenschaft zu bauen, konnte ich mit Gleichaltrigen diskutieren und auf den Prüfstand stellen. Es begann eine Art „Sturm und Drang"-Phase, die dem kritischen und prüfenden Blick des Vaters Ralf standhalten musste. Mit dem Elan des Aufbruchs und der Veränderung entstanden in dieser Zeit die ersten architektonischen Projekte wie die Eisenzahnstraße 1 in Berlin oder die Häuser am Donkwall in Kempen. Die Hartnäckigkeit und Konsequenz bei der Durchführung beider Projekte waren außergewöhnlich und mitreißend. Ralf Schmitz selbst wollte sich, solange ich ihn kenne, aus dem operativen Geschäft zurückziehen. Ich kann nur vermuten, dass er sich von seinen Söhnen hat begeistern lassen, sich weiter gemeinsam mit Hingabe in der Projektentwicklung und -durchführung zu engagieren, statt das Zepter einfach weiterzureichen. Kurzum, dass die Familie es ernst meinte mit dem „Bauen aus Leidenschaft", war über die Generationen hinaus nicht zu übersehen. 2016 begann so auch das Projekt in der Emser Straße, das mit dionysischer Kraftanstrengung zu einem faszinierenden, exotischen Haus geworden ist.

My collaboration with RALF SCHMITZ, which began about ten years ago, has been an experience characterized on the one hand by tension, confrontations and setbacks but also by many shared accomplishments. The homes created out of a symphony of economic reasoning, technical solidity and creative power are truly exceptional. Just as with any musical performance, no two houses are alike and no project betrays even a hint of carelessness or fatigue. On the contrary, over the years ever more daring and confident residences have been realized. The focus of each project remains the individual apartments, whose composition is reworked and polished to perfection in each project. Insights from previous undertakings are integrated into new designs, as are changing demands on living space, whether they stem from the recent pandemic or broader social and political shifts. Out of the initial site analysis, our respect for the surrounding neighborhood and a reflection on local building traditions, buildings are created, whose intention it is to be worthy enough of one's own standards.

In 2012, the family-owned company RALF SCHMITZ initially hired me as a visual artist to render their current building projects. "A passion for building" hung over the doorway – I was eager to find out how true that axiom was. The next generation had already taken over the stage at the firm, so I was able to scrutinize the projects with people my own age and discuss what it meant to build with passion. A kind of *Sturm und Drang* phase began, which, however, still had to withstand the critical and probing eye of Ralf Schmitz, the father. The vitality of a new era and the changes taking place led to the creation of such architectural projects as the Eisenzahn 1 development in Berlin, or the houses on Donkwall in Kempen. The tenacity and resoluteness displayed during the completion of both projects was extraordinary and thrilling. Ralf Schmitz himself, who has wanted to step back from the daily operations of the business for as long as I've known him, could not help but remain deeply involved in the development of both projects.

I can only assume that his sons inspired him to continue devoting his time on project development and execution rather than just passing on the scepter. In short, it was crystal clear that the family has taken the motto "passion for building" seriously for generations. In 2016, we began the project on Emser Straße, which through nothing short of Dionysian efforts, has evolved into a fascinating and exotic building.

Mit der jungen Generation Schmitz wurden Themen wie Nachhaltigkeit, Qualität und Ästhetik neu gedacht und in den Vordergrund gerückt, ohne sich in jugendlicher Arroganz der Tradition des Unternehmens zu verwehren. Wir sehen heute, dass wir in der gegenwärtigen Diskussion um die Reduktion von CO_2-Emmissionen fast ohne Anstrengung unseren Beitrag leisten können: Eine solide Bauweise mit genügend Masse zur Speicherung von Wärme und Kälte im Zusammenspiel mit einem stimmigen Verhältnis von Wandöffnungen schafft – ohne jeglichen technischen Mehraufwand – auf ganz natürlichem Wege ein angenehmes Klima im Innern. Die Rückbesinnung auf einfache, konventionelle Bautraditionen lässt uns heute fast wie Vorreiter bei dem Versuch der Reduzierung von Energie im Bau und Betrieb unserer Häuser erscheinen.

The next Schmitz generation is focused on redefining the themes of sustainability, quality and aesthetics and bringing them to the foreground without losing sight of the firm's traditions. Against the backdrop of current discussions on the reduction of carbon emissions we can already see how our contribution is taking shape, with almost no additional effort: A solid construction method with enough mass to facilitate adequate heat or cold storage combined with a harmonious ratio of wall openings creates – without any additional technical effort – an extremely natural way to create a comfortable indoor climate. The return to simple, conventional building traditions almost gives us the appearance of trailblazers in the effort to reduce energy costs, both during the construction and operational phases of our buildings. These purportedly new themes are, in fact, just a renaissance of values and standards that have

„Über allem steht eine Freundschaft, die aus der Begeisterung für unser Metier entstanden ist"

Die vermeintlich neuen Themen sind also lediglich eine Renaissance der Werte und Maßstäbe, die im Hause Schmitz seit Generationen im Bau bereits gelebt wurden. Unsere gemeinsamen Bauten mögen andersartig sein und dem Anschein nach den bis dahin unverkennbaren Stil des Unternehmens abgelöst haben, im Kern aber folgen sie dem Grundton der Schmitz'schen Philosophie und dem tief gegründeten Sinn für Qualität und Nachhaltigkeit.

Zu jenen Qualitäten dieser über zehn Jahre währenden Zusammenarbeit gehört auch der Respekt, die Fairness und das Anerkennen der gegenseitigen Kompetenz. Über allem aber steht eine Freundschaft, die aus der Begeisterung für unser Metier entstanden ist und das Fundament für viele weitere Vorhaben gegründet hat. Dass wir dabei auf dem richtigen Weg sind, hat uns 2021 die Auszeichnung mit dem Richard H. Driehaus Prize für herausragende Beiträge in der traditionellen Architektur gezeigt. Das Rezept für den Erfolg ist dabei ganz einfach: bedingungslose Klarheit, Begegnung auf Augenhöhe und kompromisslose Suche bei der Erfüllung unseres gemeinsamen Versprechens nach Qualität, Nachhaltigkeit und Baukultur.

been part of the Schmitz firm's construction philosophy for generations. Our joint collaborations may be different and appear to have replaced the formerly unmistakable style of previous projects, but at their core they adhere to the root of the Schmitz philosophy and to their deeply held conviction for quality and sustainability.

Respect, fairness and the mutual acknowledgment of our respective competencies are just some of the qualities that have defined our working relationship over the past ten years. But above all else, the foundation for all our future developments is formed by the friendship that has grown out of deep enthusiasm for our profession. Winning the Richard H. Driehaus Prize for outstanding contributions to traditional architecture in 2021 showed us that we are on the right path together. The recipe for our success is quite simple: unconditional clarity, always meeting on equal terms and the uncompromising search for quality, sustainability and building culture to achieve our mutual goals.

URBAN LUXURY BUILT FOR GENERATIONS

TEXT **Bettina Schneuer** FOTOS **Noshe, Christian Stoll, Sebastian Treese Architekten**

Das Wohnpalais mit Privatpark in Bestlage nahe dem Kurfürstendamm ist ein Ausnahmeprojekt mit höchsten Ansprüchen an Architektur, Ästhetik und Komfort.

The residential landmark with private park in a prime location near Kurfürstendamm is an exceptional project with the highest standards of architecture, aesthetics and comfort.

EMSER STRASSE,
BERLIN WILMERSDORF

Mitten in der Hauptstadt entstand in der Emser Straße eine Idylle mit Wasserspiel und exotischen Pflanzen: Bodendecker, Baumsolitäre und blühende Stauden prägen den Hof

In the middle of the metropolis, a sanctuary was created with a water feature and exotic plants: Ground cover, flowering perennials and individual trees shape the courtyard

Ab dem ersten Stock umhüllt den Bau ein Gewand aus Torfbrandziegeln; schwarze Stahlbalkone und Metallfenster, viergeschossige Bögen und das expressive Staffelgeschoss kontrastieren mit dem Grün des Gartens

From the first floor upwards, the building wears a robe of peat-fired bricks; black steel balconies and metal windows, four-storey arches and the expressive staggered top floor contrast with the green garden

Gute Nachbarschaft gibt ein Gefühl wie der Bass in der Musik: Er hat selten ein Solo – doch wenn er fehlt, dann stimmt gar nichts mehr. Denn er macht den Rhythmus, er verleiht Harmonien ihr Rückgrat. Hier heißt der Bass: Ludwigkirchplatz. Um diese italienisch anmutende Piazza finden sich feine, inhabergeführte Cafés, Läden und Galerien – sie bieten das Besondere, das Ausgesuchte. Das charmante Eck gilt schon seit Generationen als hochbegehrte Wohnadresse. Von dieser Idylle ist der noble Kurfürstendamm mit seinem kosmopolitischen Flair jedoch nur fünf Minuten entfernt – zu Fuß!

„Urbane Orte mit Wow-Effekt" nennt Axel Martin Schmitz solche erlesenen Mikrolagen im Hauptstadtmarkt, die RALF SCHMITZ seit 2004 für seine Kunden in Berlin sucht und findet. An so einem Wow-Ort ist das Ausnahmeprojekt Alexander entstanden, benannt nach dem preußischen Naturforscher und Gelehrten von Humboldt. Ein markanter Solitär, der die Nähe zur Berliner Backsteintradition sucht: Sein Sockel aus hellem Naturstein formuliert präzise die Kubatur des Gebäudes, Ziegel im Sonderformat mit dunklen Fugen umhüllen die oberen Etagen. Schwarz lackierte Stahlbalkone, Holz-Alu-Fenster, Risalite, Bogenfenster und das expressive Staffelgeschoss erinnern an klassische Kontorhäuser. Und lassen die Großzügigkeit der 42 Wohnungen erahnen, allesamt hell durch Grundrisse in mindestens zwei Himmelsrichtungen.

Exklusive Details wie individuell gefertigte Innentüren, edle Schalterprogramme von Berker, Eichenparkett, En-suite-Bäder sowie handgezogene Stuckprofile zeichnen die Ausstattung aus. „Speziell an der Spree setzen wir auf den Spannungsbogen Alt – Neu", charakterisiert Axel Martin Schmitz das Stilkonzept. Das gekonnte Spiel mit architekturhistorischen Zitaten ergänzen diskret modernste Wohnraumlüftungsanlagen mit Wärmerückgewinnung für ein angenehmes Raumklima.

Die gemeinschaftlichen Foyers und Treppenhäuser sind geprägt von Natursteinböden aus Nero Marquina und extravagantem Rosso Levanto, aufwendigen Wandgestaltungen mit besonderen Farben und außergewöhnlichen, ornamentalen Fliesen. Bis zu vier Meter tiefe Vorgärten schirmen diesen neuen Stadtbaustein ab und sind zugleich Vorboten eines einzigartigen *jardin botanique:* Der üppige Hofgarten mit Stauden, Gräsern und einem Wasserspiel ist grüne Kulisse, duftende Ruheoase oder privates Universum für alle Bewohner; die bekannte Königliche Gartenakademie setzte diese Idee kongenial um.

Luxus definiert sich hier als Dauerzustand: Er wird im Wohnpalais an der Emser Straße nicht nur im ersten Moment als solcher empfunden, sondern bestimmt auch nach Jahrzehnten noch immer das Lebensgefühl in einem Alexander-Apartment.

Good neighbourhoods give a feeling like the bass line in music: it rarely has a solo – but when it is missing, nothing feels right anymore. Because bass makes the rhythm, it gives harmonies their backbone. Here, the bass is called Ludwigkirchplatz. Clustered around this Italian-style piazza are a collection of wonderful, independent cafés, stores and galleries, all offering something special, something unique. This charming corner has been a highly sought-after residential address for generations. And the cosmopolitan flair of the Kurfürstendamm is only five minutes away – on foot!

"Urban places with a wow factor" is what Axel Martin Schmitz calls such exquisite micro-locations in the capital market, which RALF SCHMITZ has been searching for – and finding – for its clients in Berlin since 2004. At such a wow location, the exceptional project Alexander was created, named after the Prussian naturalist and scholar von Humboldt. The building is striking in its singularity, seeking proximity to Berlin's brick tradition. The base of light-colored natural stone precisely formulates its cubature, while thin bricks in a special format and dark caulk enrobe the upper floors. Black steel balconies, aluminum-clad windows, avant-corps, arched windows and the staggered top floor are reminiscent of classic turn-of-the-20th-century office buildings. And hint at the spaciousness of the 42 apartments, all luminous thanks to floor plans in at least two directions.

Exclusive details such as individually manufactured interior doors, switch plates from Berker, oak parquet, en-suite bathrooms as well as hand-drawn stucco moldings characterize the furnishings. "Especially on the Spree, we rely on the suspense between old and new," says Axel Martin Schmitz, characterizing the style concept. The skilful play with architectural-historical citations is discreetly complemented by state-of-the-art residential ventilation systems with heat recovery for a pleasant indoor climate.

The common foyers and staircases are characterized by natural stone floors of Nero Marquina and extravagant Rosso Levanto, elaborate wall designs with special colors and unusual ornamental tiles. Front gardens up to four meters deep shield this new urban landmark and are at the same time harbingers of a unique *jardin botanique*: the lush courtyard with perennials, grasses and a water feature is a green setting, a fragrant oasis of tranquility or a private universe for all residents; the renowned Royal Garden Academy implemented this idea ingeniously.

Here, luxury defines itself as a permanent state: it is not perceived just at one's first moment in the residential palace on Emser Straße, but determines one's attitude towards living in an Alexander apartment – even after decades.

———————

Die Königliche Gartenakademie
plante den opulenten botanischen
Garten im Miniaturformat, zu dem
sich jede der 42 Wohnungen öffnet

Berlin's Royal Garden Academy
planned this miniature botanical
garden to which each of the
42 exquisite apartments open up

„Der Anblick
eines freien, kraftvollen
Pflanzenwuchses
erfrischt und stärkt
das Gemüt"

Alexander von Humboldt
"The sight of a free and powerful vegetation refreshes
and strengthens the mind"

Prächtige Foyers mit verschiedenen
Farbkonzepten und aufwendigen Wandgestaltungen adeln das Alexander
zu weit mehr als einem großbürgerlichen Wohnhaus an bester Adresse

Magnificent foyers with diverse
color concepts and elaborate wall
treatments elevate the Alexander
to much more than an upper-class
building in an outstanding location

„Allem Leben, allem Tun, aller Kunst muss das Handwerk vorausgehen"

Johann Wolfgang von Goethe
"All life, all activity, all art must follow from craftsmanship"

SUBTLE DIVERSITY OF STYLE

TEXT **Bettina Schneuer** FOTOS **Noshe**

Das neue Berliner Showroom-Apartment
zeigt gekonnt, dass Luxus die
Fusion exquisiter Möbel mit besonderen
Materialien bedeutet. Willkommen
in der Welt des Alexander!

The new Berlin showroom apartment
skillfully demonstrates that
luxury means the fusion of exquisite
furniture with special materials.
Welcome to the Alexander!

Mondäner Stilkosmos: Die Küche
aus matt poliertem Naturstein
und lackiertem Mahagoni beleuchten
von Hand mattierte Glaskugeln
der US-Manufaktur Apparatus.
Artwork: Marcel Frey (2018)

Glamorous style cosmos: The kitchen
made of matte polished natural stone
and lacquered mahogany is illuminated by glass orbs, matted by hand,
from the US manufacturer Apparatus.
Artwork: Marcel Frey (2018)

Arabescato-Marmor rahmt im
Hauptbad die gusseiserne Wanne
„Regal Colors" von Devon&Devon,
der Fifties-Schemel von Perriand
nimmt deren Sonderlackierung auf.
Wandobjekt: Joachim Bandau (2014)

In the main bath, Arabescato
marble frames Devon&Devon's
cast-iron tub "Regal Colors," the
Fifties stool by Charlotte Perriand
echoes its custom paint job.
Wall object: Joachim Bandau (2014)

Sanfte Töne und prächtige Materialien verbinden sich zu eleganten Räumen

Soft tones and magnificent materials combine
to create elegant spaces

Traumschön: Softe Töne wie
Zartgrau, Mauve und Creme,
kombiniert mit edlem Nussbaum
und Leinen, schaffen im Schlafzimmer subtil ein Flair der Ruhe

Dream team: Soft tones like
pale gray, mauve and cream,
combined with precious walnut
and linen, subtly create a flair
of tranquility in the bedroom

Wand Badezimmer: Joachim Bandau

Stirnwand: Marcel Frey

Kurvenstars: Im Wohnzimmer vereinte Interior Designer Oliver Jungel gekonnt diverse Texturen, organische Formen und satte Farben. Tisch und Sessel lieferte die Luxusmanufaktur Alfonso Marina, das Sofa „Julep" ist eine Sonderanfertigung in Samt. Der Berliner Marcel Frey schuf den schwarzweißen Gipsschnitt 2011

Curvy chic: In the living room, interior designer Oliver Jungel skillfully combined textures, organic shapes and rich colors. The table and armchairs were supplied by luxury manufacturer Alfonso Marina, the "Julep" sofa was custom-upholstered in green velvet. Marcel Frey created the black and white plaster cut in 2011

Maximal minimal: Den Ess-
bereich prägen Schwarz, Weiß,
Grau – und Licht! Ein Bronzefuß
trägt die außergewöhnliche
Platte des maßgefertigten Tischs

Maximal minimalism: The
dining area is dominated by
black, white, gray – and light!
A bronze base supports
the extraordinary top of the
made-to-measure table

Deckenhohe, mit Ledergeflecht
bespannte Türen fassonieren
die Ankleide. Der schwungvolle
Schminktisch ist ein Unikat.
Accessoires: Michaël Verheyden

Ceiling-high doors covered with
leather mesh frame the en-suite
dressing room. The sleek curved
vanity table is a one-of-a-kind.
Accessories: Michaël Verheyden

Work-Life-Balance: Sinnlich-
dunkle Wände harmonieren
im Homeoffice mit dem hellen
Daybed (links). Großformat:
Friedemann Heckel (2020)

Work-life balance: Sensual
dark walls in the home office
work well with the creamy
daybed (left). Large format:
Friedemann Heckel (2020)

„Man braucht nicht
viele Dinge, doch was
man hat, sollte von
absoluter Qualität sein"

Oliver Jungel
"You don't need lots of things, but what
you do have should be of absolute quality"

Sie sind Inspirationen für das eigene Domizil: die eleganten Showroom-Wohnungen von RALF SCHMITZ mit ihren erlesenen Einrichtungen. Das gilt besonders für das im Herbst 2022 fertiggestellte Apartment im markanten Backsteinbau nahe dem Kurfürstendamm. Stilsicher ist auch innerhalb der Kubatur dieses Solitärs dessen Symbiose aus Eleganz und Komfort weitergeführt: Oliver Jungel, dessen Studio seit über 20 Jahren eng mit dem Unternehmen verbunden ist, erdachte die spektakuläre Gestaltung der Gemeinschaftsbereiche und war Ideengeber für den üppigen Hofgarten. Der Düsseldorfer verantwortete zudem das komplette Design der eindrucksvollen Musterwohnung: Im vierten Stock ließ er einen Kosmos in subtil komponierten Farbwelten entstehen, der gelassen zwischen Klassischem und Zeitgenössischem balanciert und die Idee des modernen Luxus neu definiert.

Aus dem Entree leiten maßgefertigte Sprossentüren aus Messing und Glas in den Wohnsalon: Hier versammeln sich das elegant geschwungene Tacchini-Samtsofa und zwei Sessel auf einem Nanimarquina-Teppich um den organisch geformten Couchtisch aus Marmor und gebeiztem Holz zu einem kosmopolitischen Ensemble von leiser Opulenz. Schwarze Schiebetüren führen zur außergewöhnlichen Insel-Küche aus flanellgrauem, wachsmatt polierten Eros-Grey-Naturstein und dunkel lackiertem Mahagoni. Das Lichtkugelobjekt „Cloud" von Apparatus setzt den Essbereich mit seinem außergewöhnlichen Triangel-Tisch in Szene. Vom Living geht es – neben dem Ausgang zur großzügigen Loggia – in ein kleines, intimes Zimmer, das als Homeoffice gestaltet wurde: Wände in warmtonigem *oxblood* rahmen den Schreibtischklassiker von Pierre Chareau und ein maßgefertigtes Daybed, dazu gesellen sich skulpturale Beistelltische des französischen Kunstschmieds Stéphane Ducatteau.

Eine weitere Schiebetür leitet in den privaten Trakt: In der luxuriösen Ankleide mit Schminktisch geben beidseitig deckenhohe, bespannte Türen auf Knopfdruck den Blick auf Kleidung und Accessoires frei. Mittelpunkt des Hauptschlafraums ist ein maßgefertigtes Bett mit Kopfteil aus amerikanischem Nussbaum und Rohseide in Mauve. Eine imposante Kommode aus geschwärztem Stahl, oxidiertem Messing, Walnussholz und Ledergriffen feiert die Vielfalt von Material und Manufaktur; zarte Vorhänge und der weich bezogene, lässige Kelly-Wearstler-Lounger „Emmett" geben diesem Rückzugsort seine Atmosphäre tiefer Ruhe. Beide Bäder umhüllt Arabescato-Marmor; im Hauptbad illuminiert eine wandbündige Lichtplatte mit programmierbaren Leuchtstufen die freistehende Devon & Devon-Wanne, dazu kommen Objekte von Villeroy & Boch und klassische Dornbracht-Armaturen in mattem Platinum.

Dunkel patinierte, lackierte Eichendielen erden überall das raffinierte Spiel mit Materialien, Texturen und Tönen, ergänzt um Details wie das Schalterprogramm von Meljac. In Oliver Jungels Entwurf finden Erfahrung und Experiment, Leidenschaft und Gefühl zu einer virtuosen Wohnsinfonie zusammen.

They are inspirations for one's own domicile: the elegant showroom apartments by RALF SCHMITZ with their exquisite furnishings. This is especially true of the apartment in the striking brick building near Kurfürstendamm completed in the fall of 2022. Even within the cubature of this solitaire, its symbiosis of elegance and comfort is continued with stylistic confidence: Oliver Jungel, whose Düsseldorf studio has been closely associated with the company for over 20 years, devised the spectacular design of the common areas and provided the idea for the courtyard garden. The interior magician was also responsible for the complete design of the impressive showroom apartment. On the fifth floor, he created a cosmos in subtly composed color worlds that balances serenely between the classic and the contemporary, redefining the idea of modern luxury.

From the entryway, custom brass and glass transom doors lead into the living room: here, the elegantly curved Tacchini velvet sofa and two armchairs on a Nanimarquina rug gather around the organically shaped marble and stained wood coffee table, creating a cosmopolitan ensemble of quiet opulence. Black sliding doors lead to the extraordinary island kitchen in flannel gray, wax-matte polished Eros Grey natural stone and dark lacquered mahogany. The "Cloud" light sphere object by Apparatus sets the stage for the dining area with its unusual triangle table. From the living room – next to the exit to the spacious loggia – there is a small, intimate room designed as a home office: walls in warm-toned oxblood frame Pierre Chareau's classic desk and a custom daybed, joined by sculptural side tables from French artist metalworker Stéphane Ducatteau.

Another sliding door leads to the private wing: in the luxurious dressing room with dressing table, ceiling-high, covered doors on both sides reveal clothing and accessories at the touch of a button. The focal point of the main bedroom is a custom bed with headboard of American walnut and mauve raw silk. An imposing dresser of blackened steel, oxidized brass, walnut and leather handles celebrates the diversity of material and manufacture; delicate draperies and the softly upholstered, casual Kelly Wearstler "Emmett" lounger give this retreat its air of deep tranquility. Arabescato marble wraps both bathrooms; in the main bath, a wall-flush light panel with programmable luminance levels illuminates the freestanding Devon&Devon tub, joined by objects from Villeroy & Boch and classic Dornbracht fixtures in matte dark platinum.

Dark stained, lacquered oak planks ground the sophisticated play of materials, textures and tones everywhere, complemented by details such as the switch program by Meljac. Oliver Jungel's design combines experience and experiment, passion and feeling in a virtuoso symphony of living.

––––––––––

Zusammenarbeit seit gut zwei
Jahrzehnten: Ralf Schmitz und
Oliver Jungel, ein Meister subtil
verknüpfter Farb- und Material-
welten, krönten ihre Kooperation
mit dem Alexander, dem bislang
größten Projekt des Kempener
Traditionsunternehmens

Cooperation for a good two
decades: Ralf Schmitz and
Oliver Jungel, master of subtly
interwoven worlds of color
and material, crowned their
cooperation with the Alexander,
the largest project of the company
up to now

„Im Alexander kulminieren für mich 45 Jahre Erfahrung zu einem Seelenstück"

Ralf Schmitz
"In the Alexander, 45 years of experience culminate into a piece of my soul"

Rasante Formen, intensive Farben:
Das Koloritkonzept der Treppenhäuser stammt von Oliver Jungel,
ebenso der Leuchtenentwurf

Dashing shapes, intense hues:
The design scheme for the
stairwells and the light fixtures
was created by Oliver Jungel

KARLSTRASSE,
HAMBURG UHLENHORST

Alte Bäume säumen das große
Eckgrundstück an erlesener Adresse.
Die Königliche Gartenakademie
gestaltet die üppigen tiefen Vorgärten –
sie schaffen Privatsphäre

Old trees line the large corner plot at
an exquisite address, the Royal Garden
Academy designs the lush deep
front gardens – they create privacy

WHITE SPLENDOR NEAR THE ALSTER

TEXT **Iris Rodriguez**   FOTOS **Gregor Hohenberg, Sebastian Treese Architekten**

Klassisch, edel und hochmodern – licht strahlt
das neue Stadthaus in einer der
begehrtesten innerstädtischen Lagen Hamburgs.

Classic, majestic and ultra-modern – the new
townhouse in one of Hamburg's most sought-after
inner-city locations shines brightly.

Hamburgs schönstes Liebespaar:
Wolken und Wellen an der Außenalster

Hamburg's most beautiful loving pair:
clouds and waves at the Außenalster

In der Eingangshalle harmonieren
getäfelte Wände, Naturstein
und Terrazzo mit aufwendigen
Stuck-Deckenprofilen, erhellt von
exklusiven Kelly-Wearstler-Leuchten

In the entrance hall, panelled walls,
natural stone and terrazzo
harmonize with elaborate ceiling
profiles, illuminated by impressive
Kelly Wearstler light fixtures

„Es rauscht wie Freiheit.
Es riecht wie Welt. –
Natur gewordene Planken
Sind Segelschiffe. –
Ihr Anblick erhellt
Und weitet unsre Gedanken"

Joachim Ringelnatz
"It murmurs like freedom. It smells like the world. Planks gone natural are sailing ships.
The sight of them brightens and broadens our thoughts"

Was für eine seltene Gelegenheit! Ein großes Eckgrundstück im seit jeher begehrten Hamburger Stadtteil Uhlenhorst erwerben zu können, gar eines nur wenige Schritte von Außenalster und Feenteich entfernt – für RALF SCHMITZ eine rare Chance, in diesem traditionsreichen Umfeld, geprägt von prächtigen Villen und klassizistischer Architektur, ein neu zu errichtendes Stadthaus elegant einzufügen und die hanseatische Baugeschichte behutsam weiterzuerzählen.

So entsteht an der Karlstraße 27 ein prägnanter Stadtbaustein: eine Hommage an das nordische Erbe und zugleich ein Wohlfühlort für Menschen mit modernsten Wohnansprüchen, die den ganz besonderen Lebensstil „auf der Uhlenhorst" („auf", weil es einst eine Insel war) zu schätzen wissen. Vier Kanäle mit Ausläufern, zwei idyllische Teiche und 15 Brücken prägen die Umgebung; die gastronomische Vielfalt und die Shoppingmöglichkeiten rund um die Papenhuder Straße, den Hofweg und den Mühlenkamp garantieren Lebensqualität.

Als bedeutender Wirtschaftsstandort mit reichhaltigem Kultur- und Bildungsangebot gehört die Hafenmetropole zu den begehrtesten Wohnorten Deutschlands; der Kaufkraftindex liegt hier um zehn Punkte höher als im Bundesschnitt. Neben der Lage haben zwischen Alster und Elbe Parameter wie exzellente Wohn- und Bauqualität einen hohen Stellenwert bei Käufern.

All das löst die Karlstraße souverän ein: Hinter der strahlend weißen Fassade des Wohnhauses mit seinem imposanten dunklen Mansarddach und den geschwungenen Giebeln erstrecken sich zehn großzügige, lichtdurchflutete Einheiten, die bis ins kleinste Ausstattungsdetail überzeugen. Klug geplante Grundrisse geben verschiedenen Lebensmodellen ihren Raum: etwa die kleinere Wohnung im Erdgeschoss mit Terrasse als Stadtrefugium für Singles oder das Familiendomizil im ersten Stock mit zwei Loggien (die auch beim Hamburger Nieselregen nutzbar sind) und repräsentativer Eingangshalle. Dazu eine großzügige Etagenwohnung mit ungewöhnlichem Schnitt, Platz für Geselligkeit ebenso wie für Rückzug – und *on top* ein herrschaftliches Penthouse auf rund 290 Quadratmetern mit vier Terrassen.

Durch die besonderen Gegebenheiten eines Eckgebäudes entstehen immer wieder angenehme Sichtachsen, zum Beispiel ins Grüne. Das große Grundstück erlaubt die typischen tiefen Vorgärten und damit mehr Privatsphäre; die parkähnlich gestalteten Grünbereiche mit teils altem Baumbestand auf Vorder- und Rückseite werden über den Sommer hinaus zu Refugien. So fügt sich dieser urbane Bau stilsicher in seine gewachsene Umgebung, weil er das bewährt Beste weiterspinnt.

Und der Betrachter fragt sich: „Ist es neu – oder hat dieses imposante Haus hier schon immer gestanden?" Ein schöneres Kompliment kann es kaum geben.

What a rare opportunity! To be able to acquire a large corner plot in the highly sought-after Uhlenhorst district of Hamburg, especially one just a few steps away from the Außenalster lake and the Feenteich pond – for RALF SCHMITZ a wonderful occasion to elegantly integrate a new townhouse in this tradition-steeped environment, characterized by magnificent villas and neoclassical architecture, and to further continue the legacy of Hanseatic architecture.

Thus, at Karlstraße 27, a striking urban landmark is being created, an homage to the Nordic heritage as well as a feel-good haven for people who expect the most modern living conditions and appreciate the very special lifestyle "on Uhlenhorst" (it was once an island). Four canals with offshoots, two idyllic ponds and 15 bridges shape the neighborhood; the gastronomic offerings and shopping opportunities around Papenhuder Straße, Hofweg and Mühlenkamp guarantee the quality of life.

As an important business location with rich cultural and educational offerings, the port metropolis is one of the most desirable places to live in Germany; the purchasing power index here is 10 points higher than the national average. In addition to prime locations between the Alster and the Elbe, parameters such as exquisite living conditions and building quality are of great importance to buyers.

Karlstraße fulfills all of these requirements with aplomb: Behind the gleaming white facade of the residential building with its imposing dark mansard roof and gently curved gables, ten spacious, light-flooded units unfold, convincing down to the smallest detail. Cleverly planned floor plans provide space for different lifestyles: for example, the smaller apartment on the first floor with a terrace as a city retreat for singles, or the family home on the second floor with a stately foyer and two loggias (which can be used even in Hamburg's trademark gentle drizzle). In addition, on one floor there is a spacious apartment with an unusual layout, space for socializing as well as for retreat – and on top, a stately penthouse spanning around 290 square meters with four terraces.

The special characteristics of a corner building mean that there are always pleasant lines of sight, for example onto the outside. The large plot allows the characteristic deep front gardens and thus more privacy; the park-like green areas with historic trees on the front and back become refuges beyond the summer. Thus, this building fits stylishly into its evolved urban environment because it spins on the best that has been tried and tested. And the viewer wonders, "Is this stately building new – or has it always stood here?" There can hardly be a nicer compliment.

Glück ist das seltene Privileg, ganz nahe der Alster zu wohnen

Happiness is the rare privilege of living near the Alster

Schlichtheit, Kraft und Größe:
Der Giebelschwung und die
gesprossten Fenster sind
eine Hommage an typische
Hamburger Formentraditionen

Simplicity, strength and grandeur:
The sweep of the gables and
the mullioned windows pay
homage to the formal tradition
of Hamburg's architecture

PARKEN

LOVE AT
FIRST SIGHT

TEXT **Bettina Schneuer** FOTOS **Todd Eberle, Oliver Heissner, Werner Huthmacher, Noshe, Sebastian Treese Architekten**

Schönheit muss auch funktionieren –
vor allem im Foyer, dem Filter zwischen
Privatsphäre und Kollektivnutzung:
Willkommen im Stilkosmos der Eingänge.

Beauty must also be functional –
especially in the foyer, the filter between
privacy and collective use: welcome
to the style cosmos of entrances.

SIGMARINGER STRASSE, BERLIN

Komfort per Knopfdruck: Ein voll-
automatisches Parksystem befördert
Autos der Bewohner in das zweite
Untergeschoss. Von der Einfahrt
im Erdgeschoss führen opake Türen
in die stilvolle Lobby mit Lichtdecke
und Täfelung aus Kirschholz

Convenience at the touch of a button:
A fully automatic parking system trans-
ports residents' cars to the second
basement. Opaque doors lead from the
first floor driveway into the lobby with
luminous ceiling and wood paneling

Nicht mehr draußen, noch nicht ganz drinnen: Das Entree eines Apartmenthauses ist ein Übergangsort. Selten hält man sich hier länger auf; man kommt oder geht, meist in Gedanken schon in der eigenen Wohnung oder bei einem gleich anstehenden Meeting. Zudem muss diese Schleuse praktisch und vielseitig nutzbar sein: Ihr Boden muss aushalten, wenn draußen Schnee und Schauer regieren, die Beleuchtung soll hell und sicher wirken, aber nicht zu grell, dazu kommen zweckdienliche Ablagen, wo man Taschen, Tüten, Handy und Schlüssel platziert, während man sein analoges Postfach leert; außerdem liegen hier die Zugänge zu Lift, Treppenhaus und Hof – kurz, jedes Foyer fungiert als echtes *workhorse*.

Bei RALF SCHMITZ wird diesem Transitraum ganz besondere Aufmerksamkeit geschenkt: Es gibt eben keine zweite Chance für einen guten ersten Eindruck. Trotz der unterschiedlichen Stilrichtungen in den einzelnen Projekten repräsentieren durchweg alle Eingangsbereiche die unverkennbare Baukultur des Unternehmens: eine Melange werthaltiger Materialien, handwerklich perfekt verbaut. Fangen wir ganz unten an: Hinter eigens angefertigten Hauseingangstüren aus Stahl (wie etwa im Ausnahmeprojekt Emser Straße, Berlin) warten zum Beispiel großformatige und extrem solide Natursteinbeläge, oft aus edlem dunklen Pietra Grigia oder aus poliertem Bianco Carrara im subtilen Schwarz-Weiß-Raster (wie im Kempener Klosterhof). Jüngst erlebte ein Klassiker eine Renaissance: Terrazzo! Der seit der Antike geschätzte Werkstoff adelt nun das klare Foyer in der Düsseldorfer Bilker Straße.

Weiter geht es mit den Wänden: Aufwendiger Gipsstuck oder fast deckenhohe Wandspiegel fassonieren nicht nur die Foyers in reduziert-zeitloser Eleganz, sie geben ihnen zugleich Helligkeit; Vertäfelungen aus honigtonigem Kirschholz werden dem Entree in der Berliner Sigmaringer Straße Wärme verleihen.

Der Blick nach oben lohnt ebenfalls immer, ob raffinierter Leuchtenmix wie am Düsseldorfer Feldmühlepark oder die rasanten High-Lights aus der renommierten New Yorker Manufaktur Apparatus, die in der Lobby der Berliner Linienstraße Bewohner und Besucher begrüßen. In einigen der SCHMITZ-Entrees ist gleich die gesamte Decke als Lichtquelle gestaltet. Akzente setzen fein komponierte Aufzugsbereiche und Briefkastenanlagen (siehe S. 80 und 151). In manchen Projekten spielt auch Kunst eine Rolle: Stille Schwarzweiß-Arbeiten aus der „Seascapes"-Serie des amerikanisch-japanischen Fotokünstlers Hiroshi Sugimoto verweisen zum Beispiel im Foyer der Berliner Baraschstraße auf deren Nähe zum Grunewalder Koenigssee. Souverän halten die Eingangsbereiche die Balance zwischen hochrepräsentabel und funktionell – und sind dabei so schön, dass man hier sogar verweilen mag. Willkommen!

No longer outside, not yet inside the home: the entrance to an apartment building is a place of transition. People rarely stay here for long; they arrive or leave, usually already thinking about their own domicile or the meeting ahead. In addition, this space must also be practical and versatile: Its floor must be able to withstand snow and showers outside, the lighting should be bright and secure but not too glaring and there should be practical shelves to put bags, cell phones and keys while you empty your mailbox; plus the entrances to the elevator, staircase and courtyard are located here – in short, every foyer functions as a real workhorse.

At RALF SCHMITZ, special attention is paid to this transit space: there is simply no second chance for a good first impression. Despite the different styles in the individual projects, all entrance areas consistently represent the company's unmistakable building culture – a melange of valuable materials, perfectly crafted. Let's start at the bottom: Behind custom-made steel building entrance doors (such as at Emser Straße, Berlin), for example, large-format and extremely solid natural stone coverings await, often made of noble dark Pietra Grigia or polished Bianco Carrara in a subtle black-and-white grid (as in the Klosterhof in Kempen). Recently, a classic is experiencing a renaissance: terrazzo! This material, which has been appreciated since ancient times, now ennobles the foyer in Düsseldorf's Bilker Straße.

The next step is the walls: Elaborate plaster stucco or almost ceiling-high wall mirrors not only give these foyers a inimalist, timeless elegance, but at the same time lend them brightness; paneling made of honey-toned cherrywood will lend warmth to the entrance of Berlin's Sigmaringer Straße.

A look upwards is always worthwhile: whether it's a sophisticated mix of luminaires, as at Düsseldorf's Feldmühlepark, or the fine fixtures from renowned New York lighting studio Apparatus that greet residents and visitors in the lobby of Berlin's Linienstraße. In some of the SCHMITZ entrances, the entire ceiling is designed as a light source. Accents are set by finely composed elevator areas and mailboxes (see p. 80 and 151). In selected projects, art also plays a role: For example, in the foyer of Berlin's Baraschstraße, tranquil black-and-white works from the "Seascapes" series by the American-Japanese photographer Hiroshi Sugimoto refer to its proximity to Grunewald's Koenigssee lake.

The entrance areas confidently maintain the balance between highly representative and functional – and are so beautiful that one might even linger here. Welcome!

———————

EISENZAHNSTRASSE, BERLIN

Das exklusiv von Bottega Veneta gestaltete Interieur der über 60 qm großen Lobby vor dem Gartenhof macht das Ankommen einzigartig

The interior of the 60 sqm lobby in front of the garden courtyard, exclusively designed by Bottega Veneta, makes even the arrival unique

MÖNCHENWERTHER STRASSE, DÜSSELDORF

Die Bestlage am Feldmühlepark adeln der gekonnte Leuchtenmix und ein nobler Wandbrunnen im Foyer

At the prime location at Feldmühlepark, a sophisticated mix of lights and a striking wall fountain elevate the foyer

Souverän balancieren alle Entrees zwischen repräsentabel und funktionell

All entrances confidently balance between being highly representative and functional

SALIERSTRASSE, DÜSSELDORF

Kultiviert: Studio Oliver Jungel mixte aufwendige Spiegelwände, schimmernde Natursteinböden und extrahohe Sockelleisten

Sophisticated: Studio Oliver Jungel combined shimmering natural stone floors, extra high skirting and intricate mirrored walls at Berengar House

TIERGARTENSTRASSE,
DÜSSELDORF

Glanzvoll: Stahl, Glas und Wandspiegel
weiten das Foyer mit Natursteinböden

Glamorous: wall mirrors, steel and
glass widen the foyer with stone floors

BILKER STRASSE,
DÜSSELDORF

Terrazzoböden, polierter Marmor,
Naturstein und raffinierte Beleuchtung
prägen den Durchgang zum Hofhaus

Terrazzo floors, polished marble, dark
stone and sophisticated lighting characterize the passage to the courtyard

HUBERTUSBADER STRASSE,
BERLIN

Schwarz-weiße Eleganz verzaubert in
diesem Grunewalder Stadtvillen-Duo

Black-and-white timeless elegance
enchants in this Grunewald villa duo

THE SECRETS OF OUR FANTASTIC FLOOR PLANS

INTERVIEW **Christian Tröster**   FOTOS   **Florian Büttner, Gregor Hohenberg, Sebastian Treese Architekten**

Ralf Schmitz und Axel Martin Schmitz im Gespräch
über wechselnde Lebensgewohnheiten,
Raumfolgen – und die Sensibilität für Abstellflächen.

Ralf Schmitz and Axel Martin Schmitz discuss layouts,
lifestyle changes – and the importance of storage spaces.

Das Ganze ist nur dann mehr als die Summe seiner Teile, wenn die Teile – im Falle eines Gebäudes – mehr verbindet als Mörtel, Steine und Ziegel. Wenn zu den sichtbar-stofflichen Elementen Weiteres hinzukommt: Herzblut, Leidenschaft, Erfahrung, Verantwortung. Erst so entstehen fein komponierte Bauten, die souverän zwischen repräsentativ und behaglich balancieren. Außen – und innen. Denn in klug proportionierten Wohnungen mit hohen Decken lebt es sich schön geborgen – und jene, die in ihnen leben, wachsen selbst noch ein wenig.

Schon seit Ende der Neunzigerjahre setzt man bei RALF SCHMITZ auf Grundrisse, die ästhetische Traditionen mit technischer Moderne vereinen: aufgewertete Entrees, lichte Enfiladen mit Sichtachsen dank eleganter Flügeltüren, geschickt inszenierte Trennung von öffentlicheren und ganz privaten Lebensbereichen. Nahezu jede Wohnung funktioniert wie eine individuell geplante Villa, auch wenn dies die Baukosten nach oben hin beeinflusst; Sonderwünsche der Käufer bei Ausstattungen und Zuschnitt werden berücksichtigt – ein markanter Unterschied zu vielen anderen Immobilienunternehmen. Wie man diese Komplexität auf Kurs hält, darüber reden zwei Generationen Schmitz.

The whole is only more than the sum of its parts when the parts – in the case of a building – are connected by more than mortar, bricks and tiles. When these visibly material elements are joined by things like heart and soul, like passion, like experience and responsibility, only then do finely composed buildings emerge that balance sovereignly between representative and comfortable on the outside and on the inside. Because in cleverly proportioned apartments with high ceilings it is nice to live securely – and those who live in them grow a little themselves.

Since the end of the 1990's, RALF SCHMITZ has been focusing on floor plans that combine aesthetic traditions with technical modernity: upgraded entrance halls, light-flooded enfilades with visual axes thanks to elegant double doors, cleverly staged separation between more public and quite private living areas. Almost every apartment functions like an individually planned villa, even if this influences the construction costs upwards; special wishes of the buyers regarding fittings and layout are taken into account – a striking difference to many other real estate companies. How to keep this complexity on track is what two generations of Schmitzes talk about here.

Ralf Schmitz stellte die Firma seines Urgroßvaters neu auf, 2011 stieg sein Sohn Axel Martin ins Unternehmen ein. Die Grundrisse eines jeden neuen Projekts besprechen beide ausführlich

Ralf Schmitz restructured his great-grandfather's company, and in 2011 his son Axel Martin joined the firm. The two always discuss the floor plans of each new project in detail

Wir sitzen hier im Konferenzraum am Stammsitz des Unternehmens in Kempen. Seit 1864 steht Ihr Familienname für Baukultur – seit wann beschäftigen Sie beide sich mit Grundrissen?

Ralf Schmitz Ich kenne das Thema schon von Kindheit an durch meinen Vater, später bin ich selbst Immobilienentwickler geworden. Aber es gab doch eine Zäsur in meiner Arbeit Ende der Neunziger: Da habe ich angefangen, mehr auf traditionelle Architektur zu setzen. Damit war auch ein tiefgreifender innerer Wandel verbunden. Die Wohnungen wurden größer, wir achteten nun auf Sichtachsen und inszenierte Raumfluchten, sogenannte Enfiladen. Die Bereiche Kochen, Essen, Wohnen und das Kaminzimmer wurden durch zweiflügelige Türen verbunden. Und das Entree erfuhr eine Aufwertung: Wer in die Wohnung kommt, der kann gleich durch eine Glastür auf ein schönes Möbel oder einen Kamin schauen. Das war neu für uns – doch wir hatten damit sofort Erfolg.

Axel Martin Schmitz Auch zulasten der Baukosten: Denn um besondere und individuelle Grundrisse zu erreichen, gehen wir beim Schallschutz und der Leitungsführung auch unkonventionelle Wege. Standard wäre es, die Küchen und Bäder um die

We're sitting in your conference room in Kempen, the town where your family-run firm has its headquarters. How long have floor plans been a part of your own life?

Ralf Schmitz They are something I first became aware of as a kid, thanks to my father. Then I went on to become a property developer myself. There was a turning point in my work in the late 1990's though, when I started to focus more on traditional architecture. With this switch came far-reaching internal changes. Our apartments got larger, we started considering sight lines and creating suites of rooms, which are known as enfilades. We linked kitchen, dining and living areas via double doors. And the hall was given more weight so that, when someone enters the apartment, they can immediately look through a glass door towards an attractive piece of furniture or a fireplace. All this took us into new territory – and also brought us immediate success.

Axel Martin Schmitz It's still a key point of difference between us and our competitors that we attach a lot of importance to floor plans – even if that increases building costs. To create floor plans that are individual and special, we sometimes have to take an

Treppenhauskerne und die Steigestränge der Leitungen und Rohre drum herum zu organisieren. Wir machen es aber oft anders.

Also ist Ihr Vorgehen nicht technikgetrieben, sondern orientiert sich an den Bedürfnissen und Wünschen der Bewohner?

Ralf Schmitz Genau. Der Grundriss hat Priorität, nicht die vermeintliche Rationalität der Konstruktion. Wir fragen: Wer will da leben, wie will er leben, was ist in dieser Lage für ihn der perfekte Grundriss? Es ist die Aufgabe der Technik, das zu ermöglichen; die Technik soll dienen, nicht bestimmen. Das kann man so allerdings nur im oberen Preissegment machen.

Axel Martin Schmitz Wir haben in den vergangenen zehn Jahren nicht einen Steigestrang einfach so von oben bis unten durchs Haus gezogen. Das hat auch Auswirkungen auf die Statik. Wir müssen manchmal massive und kostspielige Unterzüge einbauen. Andere würden sagen, das sei es nicht wert.

„Der Grundriss hat Priorität, die Technik soll ihn ermöglichen, soll ihm dienen"

"The floor plan has priority, the technology should enable it, should serve it"

Was ist der Mehrwert in den Grundrissen durch all den technischen und organisatorischen Aufwand?

Axel Martin Schmitz Seit unserer Hinwendung zur klassischen Architektur arbeiten wir an dem Thema „Durchwohnen", daran, dass eine Wohnung Fenster an zwei gegenüberliegenden Seiten des Hauses hat. Außerdem ist uns wichtig, unterschiedliche Grundrisse innerhalb eines Gebäudes realisieren zu können.

Das ist das Gegenteil von seriellem Bauen und die größtmögliche Annäherung einer Wohnung an eine individuell geplante Villa.

Axel Martin Schmitz In unserer Haltung zu den Grundrissen sind wir so ähnlich wie der Vatikan: prinzipientreu. Da reagiert man lieber ein bisschen später auf die Entwicklungen der Zeit, als dass man sich in Tagestrends vergaloppiert. Es bedarf keiner dramatisch-modischen Gesten, um Qualität zu erzeugen. Wir bieten eine gewisse Bandbreite von Grundrissen, aber alle unsere Häuser haben eine Seele. Der Grundriss soll abbilden, dass die Menschen hier wirklich leben und nicht nur eingezogen sind.

In der modernen Architektur bis in die Achtziger hinein hatten Räume oft eindimensionale Funktionszuweisungen: Wohnraum, Elternschlafzimmer, Kind, Kind. Solche Einheiten waren später für Wohngemeinschaften oder auch das Arbeiten zu Hause nicht zu gebrauchen. Altbauwohnungen dagegen können sich auch neuen Bedürfnissen gut anpassen. Wie wirkt sich das auf Ihre Grundrisse aus?

Ralf Schmitz Bei Wohnungen mit großen Grundflächen, wie wir sie bauen, wird man nie eine zu enge Funktionalität finden. Unsere Küchen sind natürlich zum Kochen da, aber dort kann noch jemand

unconventional approach to noise insulation as well as to wiring and plumbing. Here, the norm is to organize kitchens and bathrooms around the stairwells and the risers for the electrics and heating, but we often deviate from that.

So your approach is driven not by technical requirements but by the wants and needs of the occupants?

Ralf Schmitz Exactly. The floor plan has absolute priority, not the supposed construction logic. We ask ourselves: Who will want to live there? What kind of lifestyle will they have? And what is the perfect floor plan for them and their lifestyle? A building's technical services need to facilitate this; they should serve, not dictate. It's an approach that's only feasible at the higher end of the market.

Axel Martin Schmitz In the past ten years, we haven't put in a single riser that just went straight up through the house. That has consequences for the structural engineering though – sometimes we have to put in heavy, expensive joists. Others would argue that it's not worth doing.

Given the technical and organizational complexity, how do such floor plans add value?

Axel Martin Schmitz Since we started focusing on classically designed architecture, we have been working to make sure each apartment has windows on two opposite sides of the building. It's also important to us that apartments within the same building have different floor plans.

That's the polar opposite of standardized construction and as close as you can get to apartments built like individually planned villas.

Axel Martin Schmitz In our approach to floor plans, we're a bit like the Vatican – we stick to our principles. We would rather be a little slow in reacting to contemporary developments than get sidetracked by day-to-day trends. You don't need eye-catching on-trend gestures to produce something of quality. We offer a certain spectrum of floor plans, but each of our buildings has a soul. The floor plan should reflect the fact that the apartments' occupants aren't just moving in, they're setting up home.

Up until the 1980's, modern homes tended to give rooms clearly defined roles: living area, parents' bedroom, children's bedrooms. This subsequently made them ill-suited to the needs of house-sharers or homeworkers. Apartments developed in the late 19th century, on the other hand, are better able to adapt to these new requirements. How is that reflected in your own floor plans?

Ralf Schmitz With the kind of large floor areas our apartments have, you don't get that sort of over-narrow definition of roles. Our kitchens are of course for cooking, but they also allow others to lend a hand, watch or chat – and have space for people to eat together. It's a similar picture with our bathrooms: they are often big enough to accommodate a chair or a recliner – these are not washrooms in which the only scope for decoration is the addition of a terry bathmat. And we don't label any of our rooms "children's

Karlstraße, Hamburg-Uhlenhorst: Die
150 qm große Wohnung ist im ersten Stock

Karlstraße, Hamburg-Uhlenhorst:
The 150 sqm unit is on the second floor

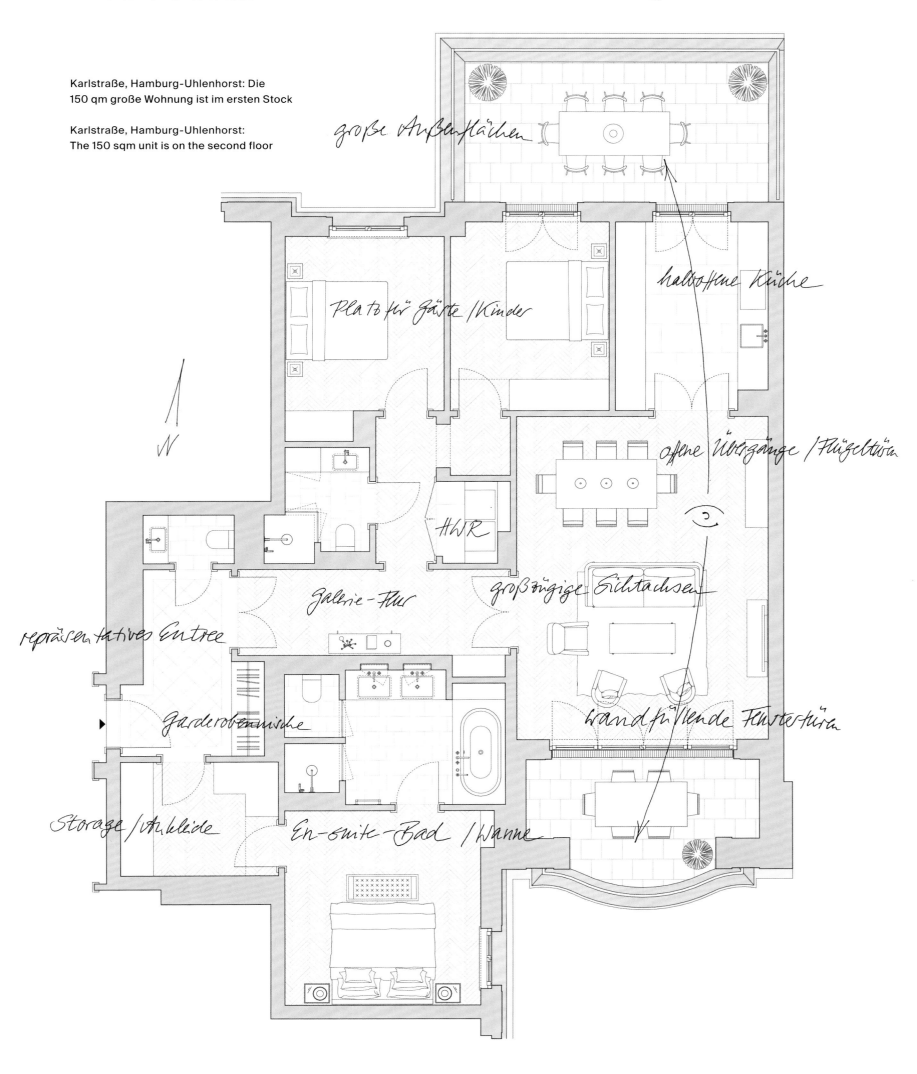

große Außenflächen

halboffene Küche

Platz für Gäste / Kinder

offene Übergänge / Flügeltür

HWR

N

großzügige Sichtachsen

Galerie-Flur

repräsentatives Entree

Garderobennische

wandfüllende Fenstertür

Storage / Ankleide

En-suite-Bad / Wanne

Das Exposé im Großformat hat 84 Seiten,
es zeigt die grüne Lage nahe der
Außenalster mit opulenten Fotostrecken

The high-quality exposé in large format has
84 pages, it shows the green location
near the Außenalster with opulent photos

helfen oder zuschauen und plaudern. Und man kann dort auch zusammen essen. Ebenso unsere Bäder: Sie haben oft eine Größe, die es erlaubt, noch einen Sitz oder eine Liege hineinzustellen – keine Waschkammern, deren einzige Gestaltungsmöglichkeit ein Frotteevorleger ist. Wir nennen auch keinen Raum „Kinderzimmer", sondern „Schlafzimmer 2" oder „Schlafzimmer 3". Diese sind aber von der Größe stets so, dass sie sich auch zum Beispiel als Bibliothek, Homeoffice oder Gästezimmer nutzen lassen.

Die Variabilität der Nutzung resultiert aus der Grundfläche?
Axel Martin Schmitz Nicht nur. Wir haben über Jahrzehnte eine sehr genaue Vorstellung bekommen, was gut angenommen wird.

Und das wäre?
Ralf Schmitz Wichtig ist zum Beispiel ein am Wohnzimmer gelegener Raum von um die sieben Quadratmeter mit offenem Durchgang. Diese kleine Fläche kommt wirklich gut an. Viele nutzen sie als Arbeitsbereich oder dort steht der Fernseher.
Axel Martin Schmitz Zum Thema Grundriss gehört auch das sogenannte Elektrogespräch. Das klingt zunächst unspannend, aber die Entscheidung darüber, wo ein Fernseher stehen

bedrooms," we prefer to say "bedroom 2" or "bedroom 3," but such spaces are always of a size that allows them to be used as a library, home office or guest bedroom instead.

So flexibility in usage is a consequence of the floor area?
Axel Martin Schmitz Among other things. Over the decades we have gained a very precise idea of what features go over well.

And they are?
Ralf Schmitz It's important, for instance, to have a separate area of around seven square metres adjacent to and open to the living room. This space is really popular with clients. Some use it as a study, others put the television there.
Axel Martin Schmitz Another aspect of the floor plan is the electronics. It might not seem like the most exciting topic, but the decision as to where to put the television in your new home affects many other things. Our clients are not a homogenous group however. A utility room is important to some but not to others. It's a similar story with kitchens. There are those for whom open-plan kitchens are a no-no because of the smells, but, for others, cooking together is a more important social occasion than the dinner itself.

soll, hat Einfluss auf vieles andere. Unsere Kunden sind jedoch keine homogene Gruppe. Für manche ist ein Hauswirtschafts-raum wichtig, für andere nicht. Ähnliches gilt für die Küche. Es gibt Menschen, für die ist eine offene Küche unmöglich wegen der Gerüche, während für andere der wichtigste Teil von Geselligkeit nicht das Essen ist, sondern das gemeinsame Kochen.

Darin klingt ein Grundthema des Wohnens an: das Verhältnis von Gemeinschaft und Privatheit. Bei dem eben schon erwähnten Annex zum Wohnzimmer zum Beispiel möchte man für sich sein, aber nicht isoliert. Andere Teile der Wohnung dagegen gelten als Privatissimum und werden separiert.
Axel Martin Schmitz Ja, das ist bei uns sehr klar. Es kann nicht passieren, dass ein Gast versehentlich ins Hauptbad oder das große Schlafzimmer stolpert. Denn auch Leute, die gerne Gäste haben, möchten einen Teil ihres Lebens wirklich privat halten.

Auch das Interieur Ihrer Häuser orientiert sich oft an klassischen Bauweisen, etwa mit Stuckprofilen. Einen gründerzeitlichen Berliner Grundriss mit langem Flur und der Küche am hinteren Ende der Wohnung wird man bei Ihnen trotzdem nicht finden, oder?
Ralf Schmitz Das kann man so sagen. Mit Raumhöhen und Stuck wird die Anmutung eines alten Hauses geboten. Aber natürlich gab es früher keine Küche, die ans Ess- und Wohnzimmer angegliedert war. Die Grundrisse von damals waren nicht effizient nach heutigen Maßstäben. Und die Lebensverhältnisse haben sich geändert. Bei meinen Eltern verbrachte man den Abend im Wohnzimmer, bei meinem Sohn sitzen heute alle an einem langen Esstisch. Ähnliche Veränderungen sehe ich bei Küchen und Kinderzimmern. In meinem Elternhaus gab es nur eine reine Arbeitsküche. Und mein Kinderzimmer war geradezu spartanisch, nur zehn Quadratmeter groß – an ein eigenes Bad war sowieso nicht zu denken. Heute ist das bei unseren Grundrissen immer dabei.

Inwieweit beeinflusst die äußere Gestalt des Gebäudes den Grundriss?
Ralf Schmitz Äußere Form und Grundriss müssen in einem guten Verhältnis zueinander stehen. Unsere Architekten wissen, dass sich die Grundrisse der Fassadenästhetik nicht unterordnen sollen. Für den Wohnkomfort nehmen wir an der Rückfassade auch mal eine Asymmetrie in Kauf, etwa wenn Brüstungen in der Küche etwas höher angelegt werden. So kann man Herd oder Spüle vor dem Fenster platzieren!
Axel Martin Schmitz Auch bei solchen Entscheidungen verstehen wir uns als Vertreter unserer Kunden. Für sie denken wir mit und voraus. Wir haben die Erfahrung, speziell für solche Details. Ähnliches gilt für Abstellräume und Abstellflächen.
Ralf Schmitz Ich habe schon vor langer Zeit eine Liste gemacht, wie viele laufende Meter an Abstellflächen bei bestimmten Wohnungs-größen vorhanden sein müssen. Das wird von den Architekten öfter nicht berücksichtigt. Wenn das der Fall ist, bestehen wir darauf, dass sie umplanen. Architekten haben für Abstellräume und -flächen weniger Sensibilität.

This touches on a key domestic theme: the relationship between shared and private spaces. Those using the aforementioned living room annex, for instance, want space to themselves but not to shut themselves away. Other areas of the home, on the other hand, are private sanctuaries and thus separated off.
Axel Martin Schmitz Yes, our homes very much emphazise that. They make sure a guest can't accidentally walk into the main bathroom or the main bedroom. After all, even those who like having people round want to keep parts of their lives private.

„Auch Menschen, die gern Gäste haben, möchten einen Teil ihres Lebens wirklich privat halten"

"Even people who like to have guests would like a part of their lives to stay really private"

The exteriors of your buildings often take their cue from classical architecture, as do interior features such as plaster moldings. But that doesn't mean apartments have the kind of plan that prevailed in the late 19th century, with long halls and kitchens towards the back?
Ralf Schmitz That's right. The high ceilings and plaster moldings help to create the look and feel you get in older properties but the latter, of course, never had kitchens that adjoined the living/dining areas. From a contemporary perspective, the floor plans of those days are inefficient. And people's lifestyles have changed. At my parents', evenings were spent in the living room; at my son's, everyone sits around a long dining table. I've seen a similar change with kitchens and children's bedrooms. At the house I grew up in, the kitchen was just for working in. And my bedroom was positively spartan, measuring just ten square meters – there was never any question of having one's own bathroom. Now it's a given.

To what extent does the exterior influence the floor plan?
Ralf Schmitz Exterior design and floor plan have to work well together. It's a recurring theme that our architects want to put the aesthetics of the facade before the floor plans. That's something we can't allow. We're happy to accept asymmetry in a rear-facing facade if it improves the living experience – we might position the sills in the kitchen slightly higher, for instance, because this allows a sink or stove to be placed in front of the window.
Axel Martin Schmitz Here, too, we see ourselves as representatives of our clients. We plan intelligently and plan ahead – we have a wealth of experience, especially when it comes to such details. That goes for storage areas and spaces too.
Ralf Schmitz I have a list I drew up a long time ago noting how many linear metres of storage space you need for various sizes of apartments. It's something architects are sometimes prone to forget. If they do, we insist that they redraw the plans. Architects have less appreciation of storage spaces and areas.

WATERFRONT LIVING

Luxuriös leben im Einklang mit der Natur –
dennoch fast am Kurfürstendamm: Das imposante
Haus Bennett am Halensee verbindet
Metropolenfeeling mit Privatsphäre im Grünen.

Luxurious living in harmony with nature –
yet almost on Kurfürstendamm: the imposing
Haus Bennett on Halensee combines
metropolitan feeling with privacy and verdancy.

TEXT **Bettina Schneuer** FOTOS **Christian Stoll**

TRABENER STRASSE,
BERLIN GRUNEWALD

Weiße Eleganz auf einem raren
Grundstück mit Wasserzugang:
Fünf Wohnungen von 185 bis 310 qm
umfasst das Anwesen, darunter
zwei Duplexe und das Penthouse

White elegance on a rare plot
with water access: the property
comprises five flats ranging from
185 to 310 sqm, including two
duplexes and the penthouse

Klassisch-zurückhaltend entworfen,
feiert das markante Gebäude souverän
die Ausblicke über das 3300 qm große
Grundstück mit alten Bäumen, neuer
Gestaltung und malerischem Seeufer

Classically restrained in its design,
the striking building confidently
celebrates the views across the 3,300 sqm
plot with mature trees, new landscaping
and picturesque lakefront

Für die großzügige Lobby wurde wie für die Außenbereiche ein heller Kalkstein verwendet, der an die distinguierten Eingangshallen von Mailand erinnert

For the spacious lobby, as for the outside areas, limestone was used, which is reminiscent of distinguished entrance halls such as those in Milan

Neue Gebäude in einer gewachsenen Umgebung sollten sich in ihren Dimensionen und stilistischen Details am Bestehenden orientieren – und dennoch eine eigenständige Handschrift entwickeln. Das gelingt diesem Bau an der Trabener Straße mühelos: Er strahlt mit seinen klaren Linien und dem lichten Putz unterm dunklen Zinkdach eine Eleganz aus, die über ästhetische Trends hinaus Bestand hat. Noblesse oblige, denn seine Lage ist außergewöhnlich – Haus Bennett wurde auf einem der wenigen und daher hochbegehrten Seegrundstücke in Berlin-Grunewald errichtet.

Die opulenten Grundrisse passen zu der illustren Adresse: Drei der fünf Einheiten – die beiden Duplexwohnungen und das Penthouse – bieten jeweils über 300 Quadratmeter Wohnfläche. Alle Apartments verfügen über großzügige Terrassen, belegt mit noblen Muschelkalkplatten, oder über ausladende Balkone hin zum idyllischen Halensee. Lang gestreckte Wasserbecken, den privaten Außenbereichen der beiden eleganten Maisonette-Apartments vorgelagert, sind quasi gezähmte Miniaturen des Sees, zu dessen Ufer sich der über 3000 Quadratmeter große Gemeinschaftsgarten sanft hinabwellt.

Altehrwürdiger Baumbestand in Kombination mit gekonnten Neuanpflanzungen schirmen das freistehende Anwesen so raffiniert ab, als lebte man in einem stillen Park – und ist dennoch in nur wenigen Minuten am weltberühmten Kurfürstendamm zum Shoppen, Essen und Flanieren.

Jedes RALF SCHMITZ-Haus besitzt eine ganz eigene Ortsidentität, die sich in zahlreichen Facetten der durchdachten Innen- und Außengestaltung spiegelt. Je mehr davon aus einem Guss stammen, desto harmonischer wirkt das Gesamtbild des neuen Stadtbausteins. Deswegen runden in dieser Seevilla perfekt verarbeitete Materialien wie Eiche-Fischgrätparkett und Naturstein in den repräsentativen Einheiten sowie wertige Bauelemente im Foyer das besondere, gehobene Wohnambiente dieser einmaligen Lage ab; die Option auf einen Kamin existiert. Modernen Komfort bieten die hohen Sicherheitsstandards, der vornehm gestaltete Aufzug und eine Tiefgarage mit zwölf Stellplätzen samt Autolift.

Mit nonchalanter Selbstverständlichkeit spannt das Haus Bennett den ästhetischen Bogen zur historischen Stadt und ihren überlieferten Strukturen – zur traditionsreichen Villenkolonie Grunewald, die ab 1890 im wilhelminischen Berlin zum Ort des weltoffenen Großbürgertums avancierte. Auch deshalb wird es auch noch in vielen Jahrzehnten überzeugen. Seinen Namen trägt dieses Premiumprojekt zur Erinnerung und Referenz an jenen wagemutigen US-Piloten, der hier am Halensee vierzig Jahre lang glücklich lebte: an „Mister Rosinenbomber" Captain Jack O. Bennett, einst Held der Luftbrücke nach West-Berlin.

The dimensions and stylistic details of new buildings in an established environment should be based on those of existing buildings – and yet develop an independent signature. This striking building on Trabener Straße succeeds effortlessly in transforming traditional vocabulary: with its clear lines and light plaster under its dark zinc roof, it radiates a timeless elegance that endures beyond aesthetic trends. Noblesse oblige, because its location is exceptional – on one of the few and therefore highly sought-after lakefront properties in Berlin-Grunewald.

The opulent floor plans match the illustrious address: Three of the five units – the two duplex apartments and the penthouse – each offer over 300 square meters of living space. All apartments have spacious terraces, covered with refined shell limestone slabs, or overhanging balconies facing the idyllic Halensee lake. Elongated water basins in front of the private outdoor areas of the two elegant maisonettes are virtually tamed miniatures of the lake, to the shore of which the more than 3,000-square-meter community garden gently slopes.

The combination of old trees and skilfully planted new greenery shields the free-standing estate as if it were a quiet park, yet the world-famous Kurfürstendamm is only a few minutes away for shopping, dining and strolling.

Each RALF SCHMITZ house has its very own local identity, which is reflected in numerous facets of the well-thought-out interior and exterior design. The more of them that come from a single mold, the more harmonious the overall appearance, the more beautiful the new urban building. In this premium project, therefore, perfectly processed materials such as oak herringbone parquet and natural stone Pietra Grigia in the representative units and valuable building elements in the foyer of the lakeside villa round off the special, upscale living ambience of this unique location; the option of a fireplace exists. Modern comfort is offered by high safety standards, the beautifully conceived elevator and an underground garage with twelve parking spots plus a car elevator.

Haus Bennett is a natural and nonchalant link between the city and its traditional structures and the elegant mansions of Grunewald, which, from 1890 on, became the preferred place of the cosmopolitan upper class. This is another reason why this building will continue to impress for many decades to come. It bears its name in memory and reverence of the daring American pilot who lived happily at Halensee for 40 years: Captain Jack O. Bennett, a hero of the West Berlin airlift.

„Ein Nachmittag in Halensee
klingt fast so poetisch
wie vier Wochen auf Capri"

Theodor Fontane
"An afternoon in Halensee sounds almost as poetic as four weeks on Capri"

Die reduzierte Palette aus hellem
Putz, dunklem Schiefer und grauem
Kalkstein lässt dem üppigen privaten
Park den Vortritt. Riesige Terrassen,
Loggien und Balkone sorgen dafür,
dass die gezähmte Natur mit einzieht

The reduced palette of light plaster,
dark slate and gray limestone gives
precedence to the private park.
Huge terraces and balconies ensure
that tamed nature moves in as well

„Viele Berliner verließen ab 1960 die bedrohte Stadt – ich kaufte trotzig mein Grundstück am Halensee"

Voreigentümer Cpt. Jack O. Bennett, Pilot und Held der Luftbrücke
"Many Berliners left the threatened city from 1960 onwards, but I defiantly bought my plot of land by the lake"

MODERN LUXURIOUS BATHROOMS

TEXT **Tanja Pabelick**
FOTOS **Todd Eberle, Gregor Hohenberg, Werner Huthmacher, Noshe, Pure**

Raum zum Entspannen, Wellness-Oase:
Formschönheit vereint mit Funktionalität.

Space to relax, wellness oasis:
beauty of form combined with functionality.

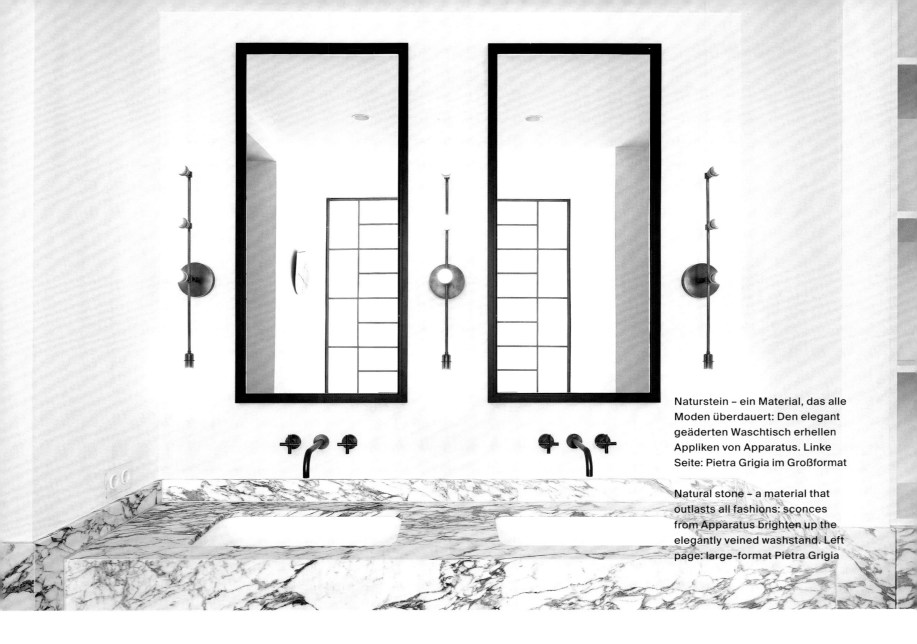

Naturstein – ein Material, das alle Moden überdauert: Den elegant geäderten Waschtisch erhellen Appliken von Apparatus. Linke Seite: Pietra Grigia im Großformat

Natural stone – a material that outlasts all fashions: sconces from Apparatus brighten up the elegantly veined washstand. Left page: large-format Pietra Grigia

In einer Welt, die permanent in Bewegung ist, wächst das Bedürfnis nach Räumen zum Abschalten. Von der alleinigen Funktion als bloßer Nasszelle hat sich das Badezimmer längst verabschiedet, an seiner Stelle laden nun durchdachte Wellness-Oasen ein, die die Grenzen zum Wohnen auflösen. Durch die Pandemie wurden die Menschen zuletzt in eine Zwangspause geschickt und waren auf ihre eigenen vier Wände zurückgeworfen. Dort haben sie neue Nutzungsmöglichkeiten erprobt und bisher wenig berücksichtigte Qualitäten ihres Wohnraumes schätzen gelernt. Als Alternative zum Besuch im Spa, als Ausgleich zum Sportstudio oder zum Wellnesstag wurde zudem das heimische Badezimmer zum Epizentrum der individuellen Entspannung.

Die erweiterte Nutzung als Rückzugs- und Kraftort brachte auch eine Anpassung der ästhetischen Ansprüche an das Bad mit sich, die bei RALF SCHMITZ schon sehr lange zur Philosophie gehören: Auf großzügigen Grundrissen sind alle Funktionselemente wie Duschen, Wannen und Waschtische, aber auch Stauraumnischen und Ablagefächer platziert und handwerklich präzise eingefügt, eine Fußbodenheizung ist selbstverständlich. Mit kaum sichtbaren Fugen und exakten Kanten wirkt das Badezimmer-Interieur wie aus einem Guss, und es bleibt viel Raum für die individuelle Nutzung. Geäderte Natursteine wie etwa der mattgraue Pietra Grigia oder silbrig schimmernder Travertin wie in der Berliner

In a world that is constantly on the move, the need for spaces to switch off is growing. The bathroom has long since bid farewell to its sole role as a mere wet room; in its place, elegant, thoughtfully designed wellness oases now invite people to dissolve the boundaries to living. The pandemic has recently sent people into a forced pause and thrown them back to their own four walls. There, they have explored new uses and learned to appreciate the previously unconsidered qualities of their living space. Moreover, as an alternative to a visit to the spa, a counterbalance to the gym or a day at the wellness center, the home bathroom has become the epicenter of individual relaxation.

The extended use as a place of retreat and strengthening also brought with it an adjustment of the aesthetic demands on the bathroom, which have been part of RALF SCHMITZ's philosophy for a very long time: On generous floor plans, all functional elements such as the showers, bathtubs and washstands, but also storage niches and storage compartments, are placed and precisely inserted in terms of craftsmanship; underfloor heating is a matter of course. With barely visible grouting and precise edges, the bathroom interior looks as if it has been cast from a single mold, leaving plenty of room for individual use. Veined natural stone, such as matte gray Pietra Grigia or shimmering silver travertine, as in Berlin's Linienstraße, is long-lasting, beautiful and

Das Bad ermöglicht stilvollen Rückzug vom Alltag und Erholung für alle Sinne

The bathroom functions as a stylish retreat from everyday life and recreation for the senses

Opulente Grandezza: Walk-in-Duschen mit Rainshower und Glastüren veredeln in den klug konzipierten Hauptbädern Start und Ende eines jeden Tages

Opulent grandeur: In the cleverly designed main bathrooms, walk-in showers with rain showers and glass doors refine the start and end of each day

Baden mit Blick in den eigenen Garten: Italienischer Breccia Paradiso in Erdtönen rahmt diesen eleganten Ruheort. Unten: Landsitz-Look 2.0 dank dunklem Naturstein, kombiniert mit Armaturen von Dornbracht

Bathing with a view of your own garden: Italian Breccia Paradiso in earth tones frames this elegant room to relax in. Below: Country estate look 2.0 thanks to dark natural stone and fittings from Dornbracht

Loft-Stil in Berlins Linienstraße:
Wanne „Kerio" von Vallone
aus handveredeltem Mineralguss

Berlin loft style at Linienstraße:
"Kerio" tub by Vallone made of
hand-finished mineral composite

Linienstraße sind langlebig schön und bringen Charakter in den Raum; oft sorgen große Fenster (und teils sogar Balkone) dafür, dass der Start und das Ende eines jeden Tages mit viel natürlichem Licht und gerichteten Ausblicken stattfinden. Separate Walk-in-Shower und freistehende Wannen, etwa von Devon&Devon oder Vallone, bieten für jeden Waschgeschmack etwas. Armaturen, zumeist vom langjährigen SCHMITZ-Partner Dornbracht und *made in Germany,* wirken wie schmucke Skulpturen zeitgemäßer Technologie auf den homogenen Flächen. Jedes Badezimmer wird aus der Architektur des Gebäudes entwickelt, immer mit der Maßgabe, ein klassisch-wohnliches Flair zu erzeugen.

Dabei ist es der Zusammenklang großer Gesten und bedachter Details, der dafür sorgt, ob ein Bad zum Verweilen einlädt. Gibt es etwas Schöneres, als im warmen Wasser einer frei stehenden Badewanne abzutauchen und alle Probleme zu vergessen? Nach einem anstrengenden Tag in der privaten Sauna zu entspannen? Oder seine Zeit effizient zu nutzen, wenn dank zweier Becken der Waschtisch zum Begegnungsraum werden kann und der morgendliche Austausch zum Ritual? Unsere En-suite-Bäder schließen sich direkt ans Hauptschlafzimmer an, fluide Raumfolgen machen das Bad mit seinen Wellness-Funktionen zum Wohnraum. Mit räumlicher Großzügigkeit, diskretem Luxus und exklusiven Objekten werden RALF SCHMITZ-Badezimmer zu privaten, immer zugänglichen Relaxzonen.

adds character to the space; often, large windows (and sometimes even balconies) ensure that the start and end of each day take place with plenty of natural light and directional views. Separate walk-in showers and freestanding tubs, such as those from Vallone or Devon&Devon, offer something for every washing taste. Faucets, mostly from longtime SCHMITZ partner Dornbracht and made in Germany, look like sleek sculptures of contemporary technology on the homogeneous surfaces. Each bathroom is developed from the architecture of the building, always with the aim of creating a classic, homely flair.

It is the harmony of grand gestures and thoughtful details that ensures whether a bathroom invites you to linger. Is there anything more beautiful than diving into the warm water of a freestanding bathtub and forgetting all your problems? Relaxing in a private sauna after a busy day? Or using one's time efficiently when, thanks to two basins, the vanity can become a meeting space and the morning exchange a ritual? Our en-suite bathrooms connect directly to the main bedroom, fluid spatial sequences turn the bathroom with its wellness functions into a living space. With spatial generosity, discreet luxury and exclusive objects, RALF SCHMITZ bathrooms become private relaxation zones that are always accessible.

Hochwertiges Material
plus technischer Komfort
ergibt langlebigen Luxus

High-quality material plus technical comfort
results in long-lasting luxury

Eine zeitlos-klassische Kombi
aus Hell und Dunkel nobilitiert
viele RALF SCHMITZ-Bäder,
hier im Düsseldorfer Greifweg.
Linke Seite: in Berlin-Grunewald

Timeless classic: A combination
of light and dark ennobles many
RALF SCHMITZ bathrooms,
here in Düsseldorf's Greifweg.
Left page: in Berlin-Grunewald

FASCINATING ARCHITECTURAL MODELS

TEXT **Bettina Schneuer**   FOTOS **Gregor Hohenberg, Monath + Menzel**

Das künftige Zuhause als Unikat in 3-D: Detailgetreue Miniaturen aus Holz verwandeln digitale Pläne in kleine Kunstwerke.

The future home as a unique piece in 3D: Detailed miniatures made of wood transform digital plans into small works of art.

EMSER STRASSE, BERLIN

Das Fassadenmodell im Maßstab 1:60 ist rund 85 cm breit und fast 48 cm hoch. Für die Sockelzone aus Kalkstein wurde Ahorn verwendet, die Fugen sind graviert. Birnenholz stellt die Backsteine dar. Alle Fensterrahmen, Gitter und Brüstungen bestehen aus Bronze, geätzt und geschwärzt

The facade model on a scale of 1:60 is about 85 cm wide and almost 48 cm high. Maple was used for the limestone base, and the joints are engraved. Pearwood represents the clinker bricks. All window frames, grilles and parapets are made of bronze, etched and blackened

GELFERTSTRASSE / AM SCHÜLERHEIM, BERLIN

Die beiden Stadthäuser von
Dahlem Duo bieten real Wohn-
nutzflächen von über 400 qm.
Ihre Geschosshöhen von bis zu
3,50 Metern schrumpfen im
Modell auf bloße 7 Zentimeter

Offering over 400 sqm of
living space, these two urban
villas on Gelfertstraße boast
ceiling heights of up to 3.5 meters
– which shrink to just
7 centimeters in the model

PETER-LENNÉ-STRASSE, BERLIN

Um den warmen Ton der Ziegel-
fassade anzudeuten, wurde
rötliches Kirschholz verwendet

Reddish cherrywood was
used to denote the brickwork
of Haus Weyhe's facade

GELFERTSTRASSE /
AM SCHÜLERHEIM, BERLIN

Ahornmodell des Apartmenthauses aus dem Eckensemble
Dahlem Duo im Maßstab 1:50.
Es zeigt den separaten Eingang
des Triplex im Erdgeschoss, über
dem sich der Balkon des Haupt-
bades befindet. Die Topografie
des Grundstücks wurde mittels
einer CNC-Fräse nachgebildet

1:50 scale, light-maple model of
the apartment building from
the Dahlem Duo corner ensemble.
It shows the triplex's separate
ground floor entrance, above
which is the main bathroom's
balcony. The topography of
the grounds was recreated using
a CNC milling machine

„Unsere Modelle machen aus Bits und
Bytes die Idee der Architektur sichtbar"

Axel Monath, Architekt und Modellbauer
"Our models make the idea of architecture visible from bits and bytes"

Ein wenig nach Vanille und nach Harz duftet es hier, aromatisch und ledrig. Dieser Raum in der Berliner Manufaktur Monath + Menzel ist das Herz des Holzmodellbaus, dort lagern Ahorn, fast ohne jede Maserung und wunderbar hell, und Birnbaum, ein wenig dunkler und auch gleichmäßig gewachsen. Dazu seltener eingesetzte Hölzer wie rötliche Kirsche, dunkles Teak oder die „Schöne Else", eine dezent gezeichnete Wildobstart. Eiche hat eine dominante Maserung und wird eher in weniger detaillierten Modellen verbaut.

Aus Ahorn sind deswegen die meisten der Architekturmodelle, die für RALF SCHMITZ bei Monath + Menzel angefertigt wurden: das Ensemble Dahlem Duo etwa, für das man auch wegen der aufwendig in 3-D gefrästen Geländemodulation über drei Monate brauchte, oder der Fassadenausschnitt des weißen Wohnpalais Eisenzahn 1 aus über tausend Einzelteilen, darunter die vielen Geländer, der Vorgartenzaun und das prächtige Portal aus geschwärzter Bronze. Für die dunkleren Backsteinfronten von Haus Weyhe dagegen kam ausnahmsweise Kirschholz zum Einsatz, für feine Details wie Stuckgesimse, Säulen oder Fensterläden und das Dach wiederum Ahorn. „Bits und Bytes, also ein am Computer entworfenes Gebilde, erhalten durch unser maßstabsgetreues Modell den Bezug zur Wirklichkeit", sagt Axel Monath, selbst Architekt, der 1985 mit zwei Partnern das Atelier gründete. „Filtern und kondensieren" müsse der Modellbauer und „aus den digitalen Daten die originäre Idee herausarbeiten" – „ein schmaler Grat zwischen zu wenigen oder zu vielen Details".

Grundrisse, Schnitte und Ansichten übersetzt sein Team in eine plastische Form. Seit der Frührenaissance setzen Bauherren und Architekten auf den Modellbau. Der geschieht heutzutage einerseits hochmodern: „Im steten Kontakt mit dem Architekten via Screenshots, Datentransfer und Online-Konferenzen wird das Modell verfeinert." Und andererseits noch immer ganz altmodisch per Hand als Unikat zusammengesetzt. Die Ergebnisse seien „einfach fantastisch", findet der Architekt Sebastian Treese. „Ein solches Modell hat zwar keinen hohen intellektuellen Wert, aber sein Bau ist natürlich ein kleiner Testlauf, ob der Entwurf funktioniert."

Das Haus en miniature ist also ein autonomes Objekt: Es hält, schon wegen seiner unterschiedlichen Materialität und der Detailreduktion, eine ästhetische Distanz zu dem später real Gebauten – und bildet es dennoch erstmals dreidimensional ab. Seine kunstfertig entstandene Form beflügelt unsere Fantasie: So also soll unser neues Zuhause aussehen – wie wunderschön.

A hint of vanilla and resin hangs in the air – a leathery, aromatic scent – in this space at model makers Monath + Menzel. There are supplies of beautifully pale maple, almost devoid of grain, piles of pearwood, a little darker in hue but similarly even in its growth, as well as less frequently used varieties such as reddish cherrywood and dark teak. Oak, meanwhile, has too prominent a grain.

Most of the architectural models this large Berlin practice produces for RALF SCHMITZ are intricately assembled from maple. The Dahlem Duo ensemble took over three months to model, partly because the varied external topography necessitated complex 3D milling. Over a thousand individual pieces were required to make a section of the firm's prestigious Eisenzahn 1 development, with its many balconette railings, perimeter fence and imposing blackened bronze entrance. Cherrywood was chosen for the darker brick façades of Haus Weyhe, with maple used only for fine details such as plaster cornices, columns and window shutters as well as for the roof.

"With our scale models, we are able to turn bits and bytes, like a computer-generated form, into something real," says Axel Monath, an architect himself, who founded the practice in 1985 with two partners. The model maker's job, he says, is to "filter and distill," to "pick out the essential idea from the digital data," a task in which there is "a fine line between too few and too many details." His team translates digital floor plans, sections and elevations into a three-dimensional form. Models are something builders and architects have been using since the early Renaissance and today's are still individually hand-assembled. Modern technology, though, also plays its part: "We liaise constantly with the architect via screenshots, data transfers and online conferences in order to fine-tune the model." The results are "just fantastic," says architect Sebastian Treese, who has worked on numerous RALF SCHMITZ projects. "Models like these may be of no great intellectual value, but their construction is, of course, a small-scale test run for the design – does it actually work?"

A miniature building of this kind is, then, a unique object in its own right. There is a clear aesthetic difference between it and the actual building, but it lets us admire the latter in three dimensions for the first time and thus allows us to better imagine our new home: so this is where we are going to live – can't wait!

––––––––––

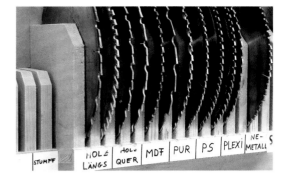

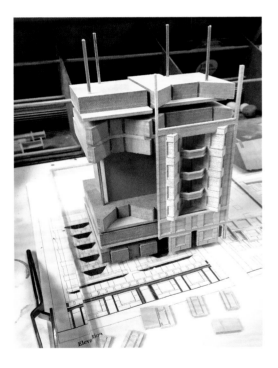

MONATH + MENZEL,
BERLIN TEMPELHOF

In der Manufaktur: Sägeblätter
mit speziellen Zahnungen; Werk-
zeughalterung auf der Drehbank.
Links: Tor, Balkongeländer und
Zaun aus geschwärzter Bronze

In the model manufactory:
saw blades with special tooth-
ings; tool holder on the lathe.
Left: Gate, balcony railings and
fence in blackened bronze

HOW TO LIVE IN A HOME BY RALF SCHMITZ

Der Kardiologe Leon Krater erzählt von Licht, Stille, Raumglück und Pariser Flair in seinem Düsseldorfer Penthouse.

Cardiologist Leon Krater talks about light, silence, spatial happiness and Parisian flair in his Düsseldorf penthouse.

AUFGEZEICHNET VON **Florian Siebeck** FOTOS **Noshe**

Die offen ineinander fließenden
Bereiche für Kochen, Essen und
Wohnen mit Kamin sind eine Remi-
niszenz an Pariser Stadtwohnungen.
Wie schwebend und daher „möglichst
wenig sichtbar" konzipierte
Leon Krater seine schwarze Küche.
Deckenpendel „Meshmatics": Moooi

The areas for cooking, eating and
living with a fireplace flow into each
other, reminiscent of Parisian apartments. Leon Krater designed his black
kitchen to look as if it was floating and
therefore "as invisible as possible."
"Meshmatics" chandelier by Moooi

Über dem Kamin: Lydia Mammes, bei der Küche: Hans Castrup

A ls meine beste Freundin mich in meinem früheren Haus besuchte, schaute sie sich um und sagte: „Es gibt Räume, in denen kann man nur unglücklich werden." Das traf mich ins Mark, schließlich hatte ich mir mit diesem Neubau einen Lebenstraum erfüllt. Ein Quader, wie man ihn aus Designzeitschriften kennt: mit bodentiefen Fenstern, einem Übergang von innen nach außen – das, was man gemeinhin als „Bauhaus" bezeichnet. Klar, zurückhaltend, so kühl wie möglich, fast museal. Das war die Prämisse. Obwohl ich lange darauf hingearbeitet hatte, musste ich mir bald eingestehen, dass solche Objekte wirklich nicht zum Wohnen gemacht sind. Man kümmert sich eigentlich nur darum, sie so zu erhalten, dass man dort morgen eine Vernissage veranstalten könnte.

Mit Wohnqualität hat das wenig zu tun, noch weniger mit der Umsetzung individueller Wünsche. Auf der Suche nach einer neuen Wohnung bin ich dann immer wieder an Gebäuden von RALF SCHMITZ hängen geblieben. Anfangs habe ich sie belächelt, Säulen und Stuck, die ans Großbürgertum Anfang des 20. Jahrhunderts erinnern. Aber je länger ich mich mit der Frage beschäftigte, wie ich selbst eigentlich wohnen will, umso stärker reizten mich die Stadthäuser der Haussmann-Ära in Paris. Oder Londoner Apartments: kompakt, aber farblich raffiniert und *cozy*. Mir gefiel sehr, dass RALF SCHMITZ sich an einer modernen Interpretation

When my best friend visited me in my previous home, she looked around and said, "Some rooms will only ever make you unhappy." This hit me hard; after all, in purchasing that house, I had achieved a lifelong dream. A cuboid like the ones you see in design magazines with floor-to-ceiling windows, a transition from inside to outside – what is commonly known as Bauhaus. Clear, restrained, as cool as possible, almost museum-like. That was the central premise. Although I had worked towards this for a long time, I soon had to admit to myself that such properties are really not made for living in. All you really care about is maintaining them in such a way that you could hold a vernissage there tomorrow.

That has little to do with quality of life, and even less to do with fulfilling individual desires. In my search for a new apartment I kept gravitating towards buildings by RALF SCHMITZ. At first I smiled at them, with their columns and stucco reminiscent of the bourgeoisie at the beginning of the 20th century. But the longer I looked into the question of how I actually wanted to live, the more I was attracted to the townhouses of the Haussmann era in Paris. Or London flats: compact, but colorfully refined and cozy. I really like the fact that RALF SCHMITZ is trying a modern interpretation of this way of living. On the one hand, my new home was to take up the generosity of Parisian city apartments – with an open-plan living-dining area, fireplace and lots of light – on the

Corbusiers „LC4"-Liege leistete sich Leon Krater von seinen ersten Gehältern als Assistenzarzt; sie ist eines der wenigen Stücke, die er beim Umzug in die Bilker Straße mitnahm: „In meiner letzten Wohnung fristete sie ein eher tristes Dasein – hier kommt sie ganz neu zur Geltung!"

Leon Krater bought Corbusier's "LC4" lounger from his first wages as an assistant doctor; it is one of the few pieces he took with him when he moved to Bilker Straße: "In my last flat, it had a rather dull existence – here it is shown to its best advantage!"

„Die Bibliothek ist einer meiner liebsten Plätze, weil das Licht dort morgens so schön ist"

"The library is one of of my favorite places, because the light is so beautiful in the morning"

Den Hof entwarfen Kessel und Züger
Architekten als Ort für Begegnungen –
ein Stück Lebensqualität, das der Arzt
in seiner letzten Immobilie vermisste

The courtyard was designed by Kessel
und Züger Architekten as a place of
encounters – an aspect that the doctor
was missing in his last property

Die Ankleide zwischen Wohn- und
Schlafbereich bietet so viel Stauraum,
dass dort – neben der Garderobe
von Leon Krater und seiner Lebensgefährtin – sogar Gäste ihre Sieben-
sachen unterbringen können

The dressing room between the living
and the sleeping area offers so
much storage space that – in addition
to the wardrobes of Leon Krater
and his partner – even guests can
stow their belongings there

dieser Art zu leben versucht. Meine neue Wohnung sollte zum einen die Großzügigkeit Pariser Stadtwohnungen aufnehmen – mit offenem Wohn-Ess-Bereich, Kamin und viel Licht –, zum anderen zurückhaltend und behaglich sein. Einer der Gründe, warum ich mich für genau diese Wohnung entschied, sind die Oberlichter im Wohn- und Schlafbereich. Sie erzeugen eine Helligkeit, die man in innerstädtischen Lagen nicht häufig findet. Das gab meiner Lebensgefährtin und mir die Möglichkeit, mit einer anderen Farbe als Weiß zu arbeiten (und mich so von meiner Vorgeschichte abzusetzen): Um die Größe des Raumes wieder einzufangen, haben wir unsere Wände in verschiedenen Grüntönen gestrichen. Denn obwohl die Wohnung im Dachgeschoss liegt, haben wir hier Raumhöhen von fast fünf Metern!

Ich hatte gezielt nach einem Dachgeschoss gesucht, weil ich in der Innenstadt wohnen und trotzdem meine Ruhe haben wollte. Ohnehin ist es in der Carlstadt sehr ruhig. Weil sie historisch gesehen das Südende der Altstadt bildet, wohnt man hier zwar still, aber trotzdem so zentral, dass man in zwei Minuten auf der Kö ist. Ich bin so gut versorgt, dass ich eigentlich – müsste ich nicht noch arbeiten – für nichts weg müsste. Es ist keine repräsentative Straße, aber eine geschichtsträchtige: Clara Schumann lebte ein paar Häuser weiter, Heinrich Heine in der Nachbarschaft. Es gibt nur 44 Häuser – aber 20 davon stehen unter Denkmalschutz. Das fand ich spontan grandios: diesen Blick auf historisch gewachsene Bauten. Und hinter der Häuserfront gibt es einen Park mit Wasserflächen.

Obwohl meine Wohnung sehr großzügig ist, schaffen die Schrägen eine gemütliche Atmosphäre. Ich fühle mich viel wohler als in einer kubischen Wohnstruktur. Natürlich gibt es repräsentative Bereiche, aber auch Rückzugsmöglichkeiten, weil ich nicht wie in einer Festhalle umherlaufen will. Den Grundriss schätzen auch Gäste: dass der öffentliche Bereich sie im Sicheren hält, dass sie nicht falsch abbiegen können. Als Kardiologe habe ich berufsbedingt nicht allzu viele Möglichkeiten, mich regelmäßig mit vielen Menschen zu umgeben. Aber als Vater zweier erwachsener Kinder, die ihre Partner oder Freunde mitbringen, ist es schön, auch mal sagen zu können: Das ist jetzt euer Abend, ich ziehe mich zurück.

Wer, wie man so schön sagt, sein erstes Leben erst mal hinter sich hat, möchte eben nicht möglichst viel Platz um sich herum, sondern eine soziale Eingebundenheit, die man in der Villa am Stadtrand nicht immer bekommt. Umso bedeutsamer wird die Hausgemeinschaft: Ich wohne erstmals in einem Gebäude mit Miteigentümern und hatte anfangs starke Bedenken – heute frage ich mich, warum ich das nicht schon früher gemacht habe! Die schöne Hofanlage ermöglicht Begegnungen: Wenn abends Nachbarn draußen sitzen, gehe ich gerne vorbei, halte ein Pläuschchen oder setze mich dazu. Das ist ein Stück Lebensqualität, das ich vorher nicht kannte. Die Hausgemeinschaft ist so tiefenentspannt, dass wir wohl bald nicht mehr von Miteigentümern sprechen – sondern von einer Familie.

other hand, to be restrained and comfortable. One of the reasons I ended up buying this exact apartment were the skylights in the living and sleeping areas. They fill the home with luminosity that can be difficult to find in urban apartments. This gave my partner and me the opportunity to work with a color other than white (and to distance myself from my previous home). To rein in the size of the space, we painted our walls in different shades of green. Although the apartment is on the top floor, we have room heights of almost five meters here!

I had specifically looked for an apartment on the top floor because I wanted to live in the city center and still have some peace and quiet. Anyway, it's very quiet here in Carlstadt. Because historically it forms the southern end of the old town, you live here quietly but still so centrally that you can be on the Königsallee (the main shopping street) in two minutes. I'm so well provided for that – if I didn't still have to work – I wouldn't have to leave for anything. Clara Schumann lived a few houses away, Heinrich Heine in the neighborhood. There are only 44 apartment buildings, but 20 of them are historical landmarks. I think it's terrific to have this view of architectural history. And behind the row of buildings is a park with bodies of water.

Although my apartment is very spacious, the slanted ceilings create a cozy atmosphere. I feel much more comfortable than in a cubic living structure. Of course there are representative areas, but there are also retreats, because I don't want to live in a banquet hall. Guests also appreciate the layout: that the public area keeps them safe, that they can't take a wrong turn. As a cardiologist, I don't have too many opportunities to surround myself with lots of people on a regular basis due to my job. But as a father of two grown-up children who bring their partners or friends, it's nice to be able to say: This is your evening now, I'm retiring.

Those who, as the saying goes, have their first life behind them, don't want as much space around them as possible, but rather a sense of social integration that you don't always get in a villa on the outskirts of town. This makes the house community all the more important. I am living in a building with co-owners for the first time and had strong reservations – today I ask myself why I didn't do it earlier! The beautiful courtyard makes it possible to meet people: When my neighbours sit outside in the evening, I like to pass by, have a chat or sit down with them. That's a quality of life I didn't know before. The house community is so relaxed that soon we will probably no longer speak of co-owners – but of a family.

Sichtachse bis zum offenen Schlafbereich: Der leicht veränderte
Grundriss lässt die Wohnung noch
großzügiger wirken. Rechte Seite:
das elegante En-suite-Bad

View of the open bedroom. The slightly
altered floor plan makes the apartment
seem even more spacious. Right page:
the elegant en-suite bathroom

„Die Bauleitung von
RALF SCHMITZ hat mich bei
der Umsetzung meines
Farbkonzepts unterstützt"

"The construction management of RALF SCHMITZ helped
me implement my color scheme"

UP OR DOWN?
OUR EXTRAORDINARY
ELEVATORS

TEXT **Bettina Schneuer** FOTOS **Todd Eberle, Gregor Hohenberg, Werner Huthmacher, Noshe, Ralph Richter**

Nur zwei Optionen bietet der Aufzug –
gestalterisch jedoch sind fabelhaft vielfältige Lösungen
denkbar. Eine Stilschau vertikaler Mobilität.

The elevator only offers two options – but in terms
of design, fabulously diverse solutions are conceivable.
A style show of vertical mobility.

Man sollte meinen, dass es bei Aufzügen keine weiteren Fragen gäbe als die nach der Richtung, als hoch oder runter, aber weit gefehlt: Für eine exklusive RALF SCHMITZ-Immobilie unterliegen die Lifte bei jedem einzelnen Projekt kritischen Stilfragen, denn geschmacklich wie technisch werden keine Kompromisse gemacht. Schon das Ankommen im Gebäude, das Erreichen des eigenen Domizils, soll schön, sicher, entspannt und langlebig gestaltet sein.

Lange war es eher verpönt, in den oberen Etagen eines Apartmenthauses zu wohnen. Über zahlreiche Treppen zu steigen, mühsam das Eingekaufte Stockwerk für Stockwerk ins noch so prachtvolle, aber leider zu hoch gelegene Wohneigentum zu hieven, war in großbürgerlichen Bezirken nicht standesgemäß. Demnach galt als die begehrteste Adresse eines solchen Gebäudes der erste Stock – die Beletage, das schöne Geschoss. Das änderte sich schlagartig, als der US-Amerikaner Elisha Graves Otis im Jahr 1853 den Aufzug erfand (den ersten absturzsicheren, wohlgemerkt).

Ein schönerer Ausblick in Baumkronen, frischere Luft und die mühelose Erreichbarkeit wurden nun weitaus wichtiger als der kürzeste Fußweg ins Zuhause. Und es dauerte nicht lange, bis die ersten Handwerker in den herrschaftlichen Bauten anrückten und

You would think that when it comes to elevators there would be no more questions than which way to go, up or down, but far from it: for an exclusive RALF SCHMITZ property, they are subject to critical questions of style in every single project, because no compromises are made in terms of taste or technology. Even the arrival at the home should be designed to be beautiful, safe and durable.

For a long time, it was rather frowned upon to live on the upper floors of an apartment building. Climbing numerous stairs, laboriously heaving what one had bought, floor by floor, into a residential property, no matter how splendid, but unfortunately too high, was not befitting one's status in upper middle-class districts. Accordingly, the most sought-after address of such a building was the first floor – the Beletage, the beautiful storey. This changed abruptly when the American Elisha Graves Otis invented the elevator in 1853 (the first fall-proof one, mind you). A more beautiful view of treetops, fresher air and effortless accessibility now became far more important than the shortest walk to one's home. And it was not long before the first craftsmen arrived in the stately buildings and provided the properties in the best locations with correspondingly elaborate and artistically designed elevators. From then on, the upper floors also became sought-after domiciles because you

Für ein Luxusanwesen in Berlin-Grunewald entstand das Lift-Unikat mit Stahlrahmen aus lasergeschweißten, gebeizten Flachprofilen – ein kühner Kontrast zum filigranen Geflecht aus brüniertem Messing und zum Boden aus Grigio Carnico mit Carrara-Fries

The elevator in this luxury building in Berlin-Grunewald boasts a unique frame of laser welded, stained steel sections and fine burnished brass mesh; inside, a floor of Grigio Carnico with Carrara frieze adds a sumptuous finishing touch

Warmtoniges Eichenfurnier prägt
Entree und Treppenaufgang,
Chrom ergänzt es beim Aufzug

The warm-hued oak veneer of
entrance hall and staircase is set off
in the elevator area by chrome

In Düsseldorfs barocker Carlstadt
fusionieren geschliffener Marmor und
Terrazzo zu einem edlen Ensemble

In Düsseldorf's baroque Carlstadt,
polished marble and classic terrazzo
merge into a refined ensemble

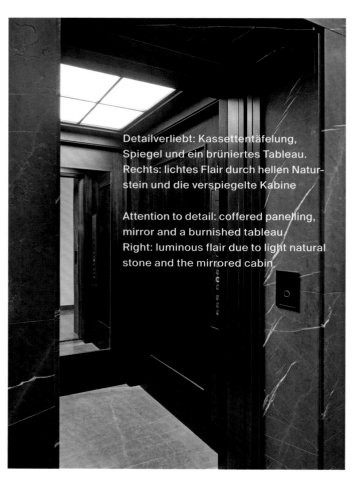

Detailverliebt: Kassettentäfelung,
Spiegel und ein brüniertes Tableau.
Rechts: lichtes Flair durch hellen Natur-
stein und die verspiegelte Kabine

Attention to detail: coffered panelling,
mirror and a burnished tableau.
Right: luminous flair due to light natural
stone and the mirrored cabin

die Immobilien in besten Lagen mit entsprechend aufwendig und künstlerisch gestalteten Aufzügen versahen. Fortan mauserten sich auch die oberen Etagen zu begehrten Domizilen, weil man mit nur einem Knopfdruck zu ihnen emporschweben konnte – speziell das Penthouse mit absoluter Privatsphäre und Panoramablick von der Dachterrasse avancierte zum Topseller und Luxusobjekt.

Was nun den Alltag der Bewohner höherer Geschosse immens erleichterte, das stellte und stellt Architekten bis heute vor so manche technisch-mechanische, besonders aber gestalterische Herausforderung: Ging es zuvor hauptsächlich darum, opulente Foyers und Treppenhäuser mit kunstvollen Geländern zu entwerfen, zog mit dem Aufzug ein ganz neuer Formenkanon ein, dessen Vielfalt keine Grenzen gesetzt sind. Aufzüge werden teilweise atemberaubend als hinauf- und hinabschießende Glaskapseln gestaltet – oder gänzlich unspektakulär als Transportmittel, das Menschen Morgen für Morgen ins Büro im 16. Stock befördert. Manchmal ruckelt man in alten, holzvertäfelten Kabinen durch prächtige Jugendstilgebäude oder springt gar in einen Paternoster. Rein oder raus, rauf oder runter? Liftfahren folgt immer dem gleichen Prinzip, doch wie geschmackvoll man sich in den exklusiven Apartmenthäusern von RALF SCHMITZ von Geschoss zu Geschoss bewegen kann, zeigt diese kleine Stilschau.

Im Berliner Leuchtturmprojekt Alexander beispielsweise gibt es in zehn der 42 Wohnungen sogar einen direkten Zugang ins eigene Domizil aus einer der insgesamt vier Aufzugsanlagen, die selbstverständlich in der Tiefgarage beginnen. Ein solches Maß an Komfort ist Premium in Perfektion (und im Alter ebenso wichtig wie mit einem gebrochenem Knöchel vom Snowboarden).

Lifte spiegeln die Stattlichkeit jenes Hauses, das sie erschließen. In einem Düsseldorfer RALF SCHMITZ-Apartmenthaus im Trendviertel Flingern ist der besonders großzügige Aufzug mit großer Sorgfalt und viel Liebe zum Detail geplant: Durch eingefasste Spiegel, coolen Marmor und klare Schwarz-Weiß-Kontraste passt sich die zeitgenössische Innenarchitektur ihrer modernen Bewohnerschaft im Norden der Rheinmetropole perfekt an. Im Theodor, dem 2021 fertiggestellten Ensemble in der Bilker Straße, wurde ganzheitlich gedacht – der zartgraue Marmor, in einem aufwendigen Verfahren poliert und den Lift rahmend, kleidet dort auch Vestibül und Treppenhaus aus.

Vereinfachte Formen, manchmal gewagte Materialien und markante Geometrie sind die drei wesentlichen Grundlagen für den Aufzug im Stil des Art déco, der im einladenden Foyer eines Luxusanwesens in Berlin-Grunewald seine Fahrgäste empfängt. Ausgesuchte Materialien wie das filigrane Messinggeflecht und eleganter Naturstein erfordern Handwerkskunst, um ein so geschmackvolles Interieur zu erschaffen – RALF SCHMITZ arbeitet daher mit einem festen Kreis von Handwerksbetrieben teils seit Jahrzehnten zusammen, die solcherlei anspruchsvollen Architekturdetails versiert auszuführen wissen.

Beeindruckend, wie ein historisches Baudetail wie die Supraporte den Sprung in die Gegenwart schafft: Schlichter als seine

could float up to them at the touch of a button – nowadays, the penthouse in particular, with absolute privacy and a panoramic view from the roof terrace, has become a top seller and luxury property.

What now immensely facilitated the everyday life of the residents of higher floors posed and still poses many a technical-mechanical, but especially creative challenge to architects: Whereas previously it was mainly a matter of designing opulent foyers and staircases, with the new technique a completely new canon of forms was introduced, the diversity of which knows no bounds.

Some elevators are breathtakingly designed as glass capsules shooting up and down – or totally unspectacular as a means of transport that takes people to the office on the 16th floor morning after morning. Sometimes you jolt through magnificent Art Nouveau buildings in old, wood-panelled cabins or even jump into a paternoster. In or out, up or down? Vertical travel always follows the same principle, but this little style show demonstrates how tastefully you can move from floor to floor in RALF SCHMITZ's exclusive apartment buildings.

Transporttechnik trifft auf Ästhetik: Schachttüren auf Maß, edel verkleidete Kabinen und Lichtdesign – exklusiv, dennoch praktisch

Mechanics and aesthetics: customized landing doors, nobly clad cabins and lighting design – exclusive, yet practical

In Berlin's exceptional Alexander project, for example, ten of the 42 apartments even have direct access to their own domicile from one of the total of four elevators, which of course start in the underground car garage. Such a level of comfort is premium in perfection (and just as important in old age as with a broken ankle from snowboarding). Elevators reflect the stateliness of the building they access. In a Düsseldorf RALF SCHMITZ apartment building in the trendy Flingern district, the particularly spacious specimen has been planned with great care and attention to detail: With framed mirrors, cool marble and clear black-and-white contrasts, the contemporary interior design perfectly suits its modern residents in the north of the Rhine metropolis. In the Theodor project, the ensemble in Bilker Straße completed in 2021, holistic thinking was applied – the delicate gray marble, polished in an elaborate process and framing the elevator, also dresses the vestibule and staircase.

Simplified forms, sometimes daring materials and striking geometry are the three essential foundations for the impressive Art Deco-style exemplar that welcomes its passengers in the inviting foyer of a luxury estate in Berlin-Grunewald. Precious materials such as the filigree brass mesh and elegant natural stone require the highest quality craftsmanship to create such a tasteful interior – RALF SCHMITZ works with a permanent circle of craftsmen

Die strenge Schwarz-Weiß-Symmetrie
von Vestibül und Lift heitern Stuck,
Säulen und Lichtdecken dezent auf

Plasterwork, pillars and light ceilings
brighten the strictly symmetrical black-
and-white look of vestibule and elevator

Vorgänger von Renaissance bis Jugendstil zeigt sich das sonst malerisch oder bildnerisch gestaltete Feld über der Lifttür eines SCHMITZ-Stadthauses in Berlin. Referenzen an die Architekturgeschichte zeigt neben dem edlen Natursteinportal auch die kassettierte Decke, die den zurückhaltend-eleganten Aufzug erhellt. Im Stil der großen Metropolen tritt der Fahrstuhl eines anderen Berliner Projektes auf. Ob es am tiefbraun gebeizten Eichenfurnier, am schimmernden Chrom oder am kunstvoll verlegten Naturstein liegt, dass man beim Anblick dieses Gefährts an große Apartmenthäuser wie in New York oder Mailand erinnert wird, sei dem Benutzer überlassen.

Sicher ist jedoch, dass sich die internationale klassische Formensprache mühelos in RALF SCHMITZ-Interieurs einfügt und das Ankommen im Domizil zu etwas Besonderem macht. Die individuelle Schönheit der komfortablen Kabinen, hinter der sich eine ausgeklügelte Technik verbirgt, passt sich stets ins Gesamtambiente aus Foyer, Briefkastenanlage und Treppenhaus ein – denn erst im Zusammenklang zeigt sich die detailorientierte und konsequente Baukunst des Traditionsunternehmens. Ausdrucksstarke Architektur verlangt nach ebenso hochwertigem Design, das Komfort und Stil bei der vertikalen Mobilität vereint.

who know how to execute such sophisticated architectural details. It is impressive how a historical architectural detail such as the supraporte makes the leap into the present: simpler than its predecessors from the Renaissance to Art Nouveau, the otherwise painterly or pictorial field above the elevator door of a SCHMITZ townhouse in Berlin appears. References to architectural history are provided not only by the majestic natural stone portal but also by the coffered ceiling that illuminates the restrained and elegant contraption. The elevator of another Berlin project is in the style of the great metropolises. Whether it is due to the deep brown stained oak veneer, the shimmering chrome or the artfully laid natural stone that one is reminded of large apartment buildings like those in New York or Milan when looking at this vehicle remains to be seen.

What is certain, however, is that the international classic design language blends effortlessly into RALF SCHMITZ interiors and makes arriving at the domicile something special. The individual beauty of these comfortable cabins, behind which sophisticated technology is hidden, always matches the overall ambience of the foyer, letterbox system and staircase – because it is only in this harmony that the uncompromisingly detail-oriented consistency of our architecture becomes apparent.

Komfort mit Klasse:
Jeder Lift passt
zum Gesamtambiente
des Hauses

Comfort with class: every elevator matches the
overall ambience of the house

Dunkle Opulenz in Düsseldorf-
Golzheim: Ausgesuchter Naturstein
in strenger Geometrie unter der
vornehm betonten Deckenleuchte

Dark opulence of natural stone in
strict geometry with accentuated
ceiling light in Düsseldorf-Golzheim

RENDERING & REALITY

TEXT **Ina Marie Kühnast**

FOTOS **Gregor Hohenberg, Noshe, Ralph Richter, Christian Stoll, Sebastian Treese Architekten**

Visualisierungen der Architekturen
von RALF SCHMITZ sind faszinierende
Illusionen – die fertigen Bauwerke
entsprechen perfekt ihrem
am Computer entstandenen Bild.

A trick of the eye? RALF SCHMITZ's
digital renderings are so convincing
that it can be hard to tell
images and actual buildings apart.

EMSER STRASSE, BERLIN

Ehemals eine halb fertige Computervision
in Cinema 4D, nun ein prächtiges Foyer:
Im Alexander begrüßen extravaganter
Rosso Levanto am Boden und raffinierte
polygonale Wandfliesen von Ogassian

Once a half-finished computer vision
in Cinema 4D, now a magnificent foyer:
The Alexander features extravagant
Rosso Levanto on the floor and refined
polygonal wall tiles from Ogassian

CHARLOTTE-NIESE-STRASSE, HAMBURG

Hanseatisch-gediegen: Backsteinkunst und Sprossenfenster unter dem sanft geschwungenen Mansarddach – die neuen Bewohner dieser Villa müssen sich nun nur noch für Terrassenmobiliar und ihren Blumenschmuck entscheiden

Typically Hanseatic clinker bricks and muntin windows under the gently curved mansard roof became reality – now, the new residents of this villa in a beautiful suburb on the Elbe must only decide on outdoor furniture and flower plantings

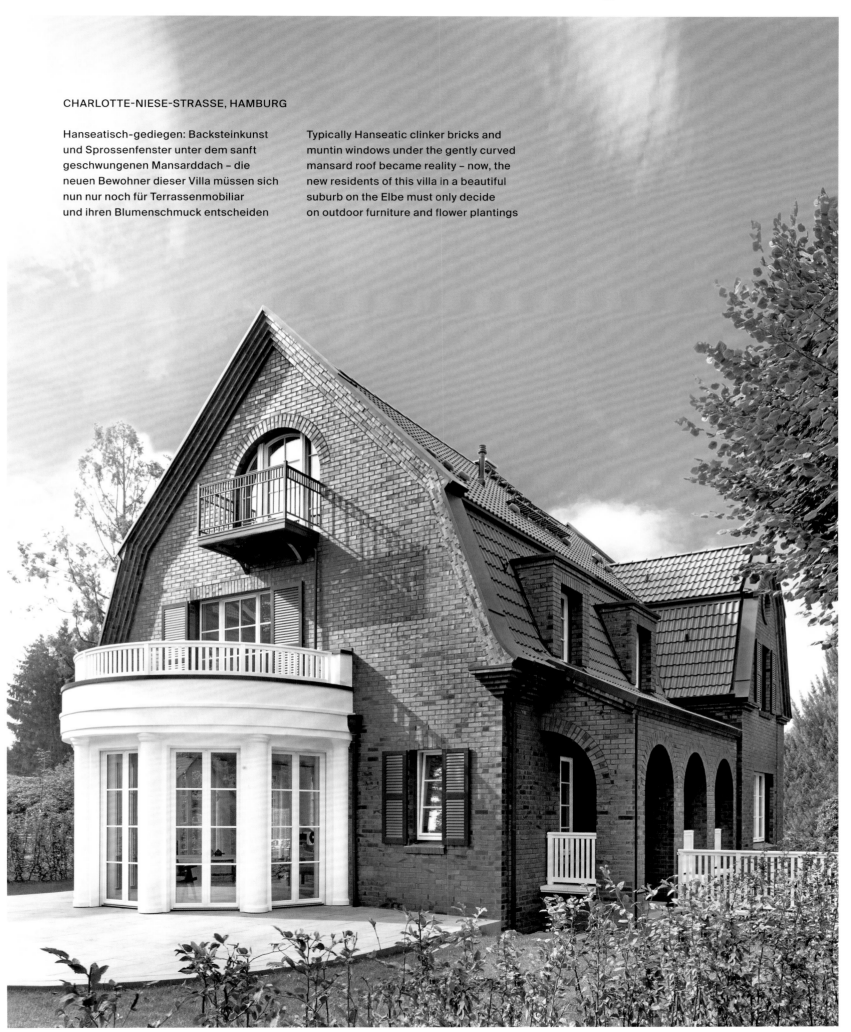

Rechte Seite: Mäandernde Erker,
elegante Bogenfenster und tiefe
Loggien geben den Blick auf ehr-
würdige Platanen frei. Nur die
Hortensien in den Vorgärten
müssen noch ein wenig wachsen

Right page: Undulating bay windows,
elegantly arched windows and deeply
set loggias look out onto old plane
trees – only the hydrangeas in the front
gardens still need to grow a bit

Der Betrachter wird auf feine Details aufmerksam, die Atmosphäre erzeugen

Subtle details that create a particular ambience catch the beholder's eye

LINIENSTRASSE, BERLIN

Die weiße Kalksteinfassade mit matt-
schwarzen Metallfenstern verleiht
dem neuen Stadtbaustein seine subtile
Eleganz – lediglich die Türgriffe weichen
von der ursprünglichen Planung ab

The white limestone facade with matte
black metal windows lends this new
landmark building its reduced elegance –
only the door handles on the first floor
deviate from the original planning

PREUSSENALLEE, BERLIN

Die berühmte Liebermann-Villa am Wannsee stand Pate für dieses wertbeständige Haus in bester Westend-Lage – links als Rendering, rechts real

The famous Liebermann Villa on Wannsee was the inspiration for this building; a solid investment property in a prime Berlin location – on the left as a rendering, on the right in reality

BILKER STRASSE, DÜSSELDORF

Fiktion oder Fakt? Die Rankpflanzen und der Hofbaum verraten es: Oben das an die einstige Remise erinnernde reale Hofhaus mit fünf Wohnungen, unten dessen geplante Ansicht

Fiction or fact? The climbing plants and the new tree give it away: the courtyard house with five apartments, reminiscent of the former coach house; below, its planned view

Ein jeder, der sie betrachtet, erliegt ihrer Täuschung. Ist die Wolke am Himmel echt, also ein Foto? Oder doch am Bildschirm entstanden? Und was ist mit dem Laub auf dem Bürgersteig, dem charmanten Oldtimer vor dem Haus? Man möchte sich die Augen reiben, so gestochen real wirken gekonnte Visualisierungen.

Die gezeichnete Welt, die hohe Kunst der Illusion, übt seit jeher eine große Faszination auf ihre Betrachter aus. Bereits im 5. Jahrhundert v. Chr. sollen Maler auf einem Wandbild Trauben so täuschend echt dargestellt haben, dass Vögel nach den 2-D-Früchten pickten. Aber auch gezeichnete Architekturwelten blicken auf eine lange Tradition zurück. In der zweiten Hälfte des Barocks trugen Architekten wie Giambattista Piranesi dazu bei, dass die Qualitäten ihrer Zeichnungen in Konkurrenz zur reinen Malerei traten.

Aber was steckt hinter der illusionistischen Architektur-darstellung von heute? In erster Linie dient sie dem Entwerfer als Modell, so wie einst die klassische Zeichnung, denn mit jeder Verbildlichung gibt man künftigen Eigentümern ein Versprechen: dass sie schon lange vor Fertigstellung der Immobilie wissen, wie diese aussehen wird.

Eine Architekturvisualisierung kann jedoch noch viel mehr: Der Betrachter wird auf feine Details aufmerksam, die Atmosphäre erzeugen und ein Gefühl für das Gebäude schaffen. Er kann sich vorstellen, Teil der Szenerie zu werden. Allerdings erfordert diese komplexe Bild-Erstellung ein großes technisches Können, zudem sollte man kompositorische und kunsthisto-rische Zusammenhänge kennen. Im besten Falle kommt dann etwas heraus, das auch losgelöst vom eigentlichen Sujet – der Darstellung des ungebauten Entwurfs – eigenständig, schön und vor allem authentisch ist.

All das schafft nur eine gelungene Visualisierung. Sie steht für die persönliche Handschrift und Sprache des Architekten und des Bauträgers. In ihrer herausragenden Qualität spiegelt sich auch die Qualität des Bauvorhabens wider. Und sie hat der klassischen Handzeichnung voraus, dass bestimmte Aspekte des Entwurfs am noch imaginären Bau besonders veranschaulicht werden können. Naturalistisch visualisiert lassen sich Perspek-tiven, Raumfolgen oder die Einpassung des Entwurfs in seine Umgebung wiederholt prüfen und nötigenfalls verbessern. Die Ästhetik guter Renderings beeinflusst sogar die Architektur-fotografie, die sich vermehrt an Visualisierungen orientiert und die Unterschiede zwischen fiktiv und faktisch immer mehr verschwimmen lässt.

Aber zurück zum Versprechen: Wenn man Fiktion perfekt in gebaute Realität umsetzt, dann hat man sein Wort als Bauträger mehr als gehalten, oder? Schauen Sie gern genau hin!

Photograph or computer-generated image? It can be almost impossible to tell the difference. Is that an actual cloud? And what about the leaves on the pavement, or the classic car parked out front? Professional renderings look so real, so convincing, that they will have you rubbing your eyes in disbelief.

The world of visual art and trompe l'oeil has long held a particular kind of fascination. As early as the 5th century BC, skilled artists were said to have painted a mural of grapes so lifelike that birds attempted to pick the fruit. Architectural visualizations, too, have a long tradition, especially in the Late Baroque period.

What, then, of today's architectural illusions? As with traditional technical drawings, their primary purpose is to model the author's plans and to thus serve as a form of customer guarantee – a guarantee that buyers know, long before completion, what they are getting. But they have other benefits too: they can also be used to draw attention to subtle details that add character and to give a feel for the overall design, allowing would-be owners to picture themselves in the visualized scene.

Generating such complex images, however, requires a high degree of technical skill as well as an understanding of various compositional and art historical aspects. Done well, they have an appeal that goes beyond their actual purpose – the depiction of an as-yet-unbuilt design – with a character, aesthetic quality and, above all, an authenticity that is all their own. Such highly accomplished renderings not only faithfully convey the signature style and formal language of the architect and developer, they also reflect the exceptional quality buyers can expect from the finished property.

Compared to hand-drawn visualizations, they have the advantage of enabling certain aspects of the design to be highlighted in a naturalistic fashion, meaning perspectives, layouts and the integration within the surroundings can be checked again and again and improved where necessary. The aesthetic of high-quality renderings has even impacted on architectural photography, thus blurring the lines between the envisaged and the actual even further.

If reality mirrors the rendering, then the developer has surely delivered exactly what they promised. See for yourself!

———————

TRABENER STRASSE, BERLIN

Südfassade zum See! Der fulminante, L-förmige Bau in Grunewald am Hang zum Halensee wurde mittels einer Drohne fotografiert. Linke Seite: seine detaillierte Visualisierung

South-facing with a lake view! The striking, L-shaped building overlooking Halensee in Grunewald was photographed with a drone — its rendering is on the left page

Der Betrachter kann sich vorstellen, Teil der Szenerie zu werden

Renderings allow viewers to picture themselves in the depicted scene

ACHENBACHSTRASSE,
DÜSSELDORF

Liebe zum Detail: Prägnante
Gesimse, per Hand brünierte
Wandleuchten, maßgefertigte
Briefkastenanlage aus Messing –
nur die Deckenkamera verrät,
was Foto ist und was die Vorlage

Attention to detail: striking
cornices, hand-finished wall
lights, custom-made brass
letterboxes – only the camera
lens reveals what is the finished
foyer as opposed to its proposal

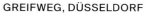

GREIFWEG, DÜSSELDORF

Noblesse, neuzeitlich interpretiert: Die
luxuriöse Natursteinfassade, gerahmt von
weißen Stuckbauten, erinnert an Adolf
Loos, Österreichs Modernistenlegende.
Das Rennrad parkt auf vielen Renderings

Noblesse, interpreted in a modern way:
The luxurious stone facade, framed by
white stucco buildings, is reminiscent of
Austrian modernist legend Adolf Loos.
The racing bike parks on many renderings

HEINSBERGSTRASSE,
DÜSSELDORF

Raffiniert verzahntes Wohnungs-
quartett im historischen Stadtkern

Cleverly interlocking quartet of apartments in the historic city center

FUTURE HERITAGE

Auf Traditionen gegründet – für die Zukunft gebaut:
Die Entwürfe von Sebastian Treese für RALF SCHMITZ prägt ein
reiches Verständnis klassischer Formensprache;
seine Gebäude fügen sich souverän ins Stadtbild.

Founded on traditions – built for the future: Sebastian Treese's
designs for RALF SCHMITZ are characterized by a rich
understanding of classical formal language; his buildings blend
confidently into the cityscape.

TEXT **Rainer Haubrich**   FOTOS **Sebastian Treese Architekten, Matthias Ziegler**

W as sind die Prägungen und Erfahrungen, die aus einem 1977 geborenen Mann einen der führenden Architekten klassischer Baukunst in Deutschland machen? Sebastian Treese wuchs in Mainz auf, inmitten einer Region, die vom römischen Erbe, von romanischen Kathedralen und Barockschlössern geprägt ist. Durch familiäre Bindungen in die Normandie war er schon früh auch mit der französischen Kultur vertraut.

Er gehört nicht zu jenen Menschen, die schon immer davon träumten, Stararchitekt zu werden und das Metier neu zu erfinden. Eher ungeplant kam er zur Architektur; sein kreatives Talent entdeckte er, als er am Gymnasium ein Bühnenbild entwerfen sollte: Die Banalität der modernen Turnhalle beantwortete er mit einem schwarzen Raum, in dessen Mitte eine klassische Säule stand, von ihm aus Pappmaché geformt. Zum Studieren ging er nach Berlin, in den Neunzigern die aufregendste Großbaustelle und mit einem reichen, aber kaputten Erbe gesegnet. Nach dem Studium an der Universität der Künste bei den Modernisten Benedict Tonon und Adolf Krischanitz suchte er sich für den Einstieg eines der führenden traditionsorientierten Büros aus: Hilmer & Sattler. Es folgten vier Jahre bei Hans Kollhoff, bevor er 2011 sein eigenes Büro gründete, lange beheimatet in einer Kreuzberger Fabriketage. Ein Jahr später kam seine Frau Julia als Partnerin dazu, die in Weimar, Paris und Zürich studiert hat.

Anfangs machte Treese sich einen Namen, indem er Projekte anderer Architekten in Visualisierungen umsetzte, die viel sinnlicher

What are the imprints and experiences that turn a man born in 1977 into one of Germany's leaders of classical architecture? Sebastian Treese grew up in Mainz, in the middle of a region marked by Roman heritage, Romanesque cathedrals and Baroque castles. Through family ties to Normandy, he was also familiar with French culture.

Treese is not one of those people who always dreamed of becoming a star architect, reinventing the profession. He came to architecture rather unplanned, discovering his creative talent when asked to design a stage set at his high school: He answered the banality of the modern gymnasium with a black room plus a classical column in the center, sculpted by him out of papier-mâché. For his studies he went to Berlin, in the 1990's the most exciting large-scale construction site and blessed with a rich but broken heritage. After the University of

„Das Konzept des Wiederentdeckens und Wiederverwendens finde ich sehr zeitgenössisch"

"I find the concept of rediscovering and reusing very contemporary"

the Arts with modernists Benedict Tonon and Adolf Krischanitz, he sought out one of the leading tradition-oriented offices to start with: Hilmer & Sattler. Four years with Hans Kollhoff followed before he founded his office in 2011, long based in a former factory in Kreuzberg. A year later, his wife Julia joined as a partner, having studied in Weimar, Paris and Zurich.

Initially, Treese made a name for himself by translating other architects' projects into visualizations that looked much more sensual than the standard. This brought him to the attention of RALF SCHMITZ, for whom he designed his first Schinkel-inspired villa and worked exclusively for a time starting in 2013. Treese became known to a wider audience with the elegant, turn-of-the-century Paris-inspired apartment building for RALF SCHMITZ on Eisenzahnstraße near Kurfürstendamm.

"I just want to build good houses," Treese says – ones that don't follow some fashion you get tired of after a few years, but are com-

Sebastian Treese entwirft seit 2013 für RALF SCHMITZ klassisch-schöne Wohnbauten. Für sie wurde er 2021 mit dem renommierten US-amerikanischen Driehaus-Preis geehrt

Since 2013, Sebastian Treese designs for RALF SCHMITZ. For these classically beautiful residential buildings, he was awarded the prestigious Driehaus Prize in 2021

waren als der Standard. So wurde RALF SCHMITZ auf ihn aufmerksam, für den er seine erste, von Schinkel inspirierte Villa entwarf und ab 2013 eine Zeit lang exklusiv arbeitete. Einem breiteren Publikum wurde Treese bekannt mit dem eleganten, vom Paris der Jahrhundertwende inspirierten Apartmenthaus für RALF SCHMITZ in der Eisenzahnstraße beim Kurfürstendamm.

„Ich will einfach gute Häuser bauen", sagt Treese – Häuser also, die nicht irgendeiner Mode folgen, an der man sich nach ein paar Jahren sattgesehen hat, sondern die einer Wohnlichkeit verpflichtet sind, in der sich Menschen gut aufgehoben fühlen. Bei der Arbeit achtet sein Büro auf die städtische Form und bemüht sich, die Umgebung zu bestätigen und aufzuwerten. Treeses Gebäude greifen lokale Traditionen auf und verleihen ihnen mit raffinierten Details universelle Anziehungskraft. Gleichzeitig engagiert er sich für die innovative Verwendung traditioneller Materialien und Techniken.

Die außergewöhnliche Qualität seiner Entwürfe hat sich inzwischen international herumgesprochen. Seit 2016 ist er Kontaktarchitekt des renommierten New Yorker Büros Robert A. M. Stern. Im Februar 2021 erhielt Treese – als erster Deutscher – den weltweit höchstdotierten internationalen Architekturpreis, den Richard H. Driehaus Prize, eine Auszeichnung für herausragende Leistungen auf dem Feld moderner klassischer Architektur.

So schwer es sein mag, in Deutschland ein harmonisches Verhältnis zur Vergangenheit zu haben: Die SCHMITZ-Entwürfe Treeses beleben eine traditionelle Formensprache eloquent wieder, die sich im Jetzt und für kommende Generationen bewähren wird.

mitted to a livability that makes people feel comfortable. At work, his office pays attention to the urban form and strives to affirm and enhance the surroundings. Treese's buildings embrace local traditions and add universal appeal with refined details. At the same time, he is committed to the innovative use of traditional materials and techniques.

The exceptional quality of his designs has now spread internationally. Since 2016, he has been the contact architect for the renowned New York firm Robert A.M. Stern. In February 2021, Treese became the first German to receive the world's most prestigious international architecture prize, the Richard H. Driehaus Prize, an award for excellence in the field of modern classical architecture.

As difficult as it may be to have an idyllic relationship with the past in Germany, Treese's projects for RALF SCHMITZ succeed in reviving an eloquent, traditional formal language that will stand the test of time in the now and for generations to come.

CHARLOTTE-NIESE-
STRASSE, HAMBURG

Das Villenensemble im schönsten
der Elbvororte interpretiert den
Arts-and-Crafts-Landhausstil
neu. Verspielte Baudetails lockern
die Geschlossenheit der Bau-
körper aus Wittmunder Backstein
in einem Mix aus den Sortierungen
Nr. 172 und 191D auf

The ensemble in the most
beautiful of the Elbe suburbs
reinterprets the Arts and Crafts
country house. Playful small
elements soften its unity, clad in
a Wittmunder bricks mix of grades
Nos. 172 and 191D

THE
BEAUTY
OF
BRICKS

TEXT **Rainer Haubrich**   FOTOS **Gregor Hohenberg, Klinkerwerke Wittmund GmbH, Noshe, Ralph Richter**

So aufregend attraktiv kann ein uralter Werkstoff aussehen:
Backstein! Das Naturprodukt mit nahezu ewigem Leben und vielen
Rot-Nuancen erlebt bei RALF SCHMITZ eine furiose Renaissance.

How exciting and attractive an ancient material can look: brick!
The natural product with almost eternal life and many shades
of red is experiencing a magnificent renaissance at RALF SCHMITZ.

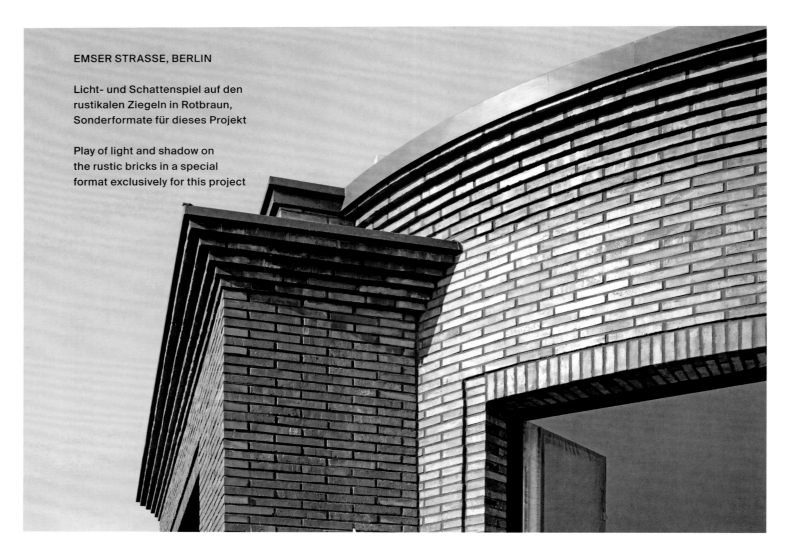

EMSER STRASSE, BERLIN

Licht- und Schattenspiel auf den
rustikalen Ziegeln in Rotbraun,
Sonderformate für dieses Projekt

Play of light and shadow on
the rustic bricks in a special
format exclusively for this project

**RUBENSSTRASSE,
DÜSSELDORF**

Weiße Ornamentierungen zieren
die Fassade des giebelständigen
Quintetts aus Klinkern Nr. 27, für
einen rustikalen Look mit der
rauen Seite nach außen verlegt

White ornamentations purfle this
front-gabled quintet made of
clinker bricks No. 27, which were
laid here with the rough side
facing outward for a rustic effect

**HEINSBERGSTRASSE,
DÜSSELDORF**

Rechte Seite: Ein Treppengiebel
krönt das Eckgebäude mit
vier raffinierten Wohnungen

A stepped gable crowns the
corner building with four flats

WITTMUNDER KLINKERWERK,
NEUSCHOO

Unikate aus Ostfriesland: Die
Ziegelei, gegründet 1860, nutzt
Ton aus der Region für ihre
Klinker, Pflaster- und Formsteine
von herausragender Qualität

Unique products from East Frisia:
The brickyard, founded in 1860,
uses clay from the region for its
clinker, paving stones and shaped
bricks of outstanding quality

„Perfekte, glatte Backsteine
können wir nicht – dafür
haben unsere Unikate Charme"

Torsten Gilbers, Prokurist Wittmunder Klinker
*"We can't produce perfect and smooth bricks – however,
our unique pieces have charm"*

Bei etwa 1200 Grad werden die
Ton-Rohlinge bis zu sieben
Tage im Tunnelofen gebrannt

At about 1,200 degrees Celsius,
the clay blanks are fired for
up to seven days in a tunnel kiln

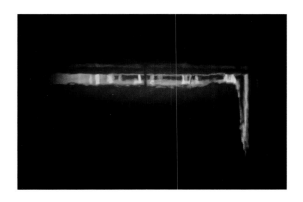

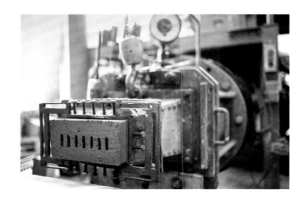

Keine chemischen Zusätze,
keine Engoben: Wittmunder
Klinker sind Naturprodukte –
authentisch, schön anzusehen
und besonders langlebig

No chemical additives, no
engobes: Wittmund clinker
bricks are natural products –
authentic, beautiful to look
at and particularly durable

Hand und Werk, Tradition und
Innovation: Die Klinker, in
acht verschiedenen Formaten
und auf Wunsch in Sondergrößen
erhältlich, werden handsortiert

Artisanry, tradition and innovation: Available in eight different
formats plus, upon request, in
special sizes, the ready-fired
bricks are all sorted by hand

HEINSBERGSTRASSE, DÜSSELDORF

Für das 2018 fertiggestellte
Ensemble in Niederkassel
nahe dem Rheinufer wurde die
Sortierung Nr. 211 verwendet

For the ensemble completed
in 2018 in Niederkassel near the
Rhine, grade No. 211 was used

Farbenspiel trifft Verlegekunst:
Zinnober, Purpurviolett oder
Rotbraun schimmern die Steine;
bei den Fugen und dem Verband
sind erfahrene Fachleute gefragt

Play of colors meets the art of
bricklaying: The bricks shimmer
in vermilion, purple violet
or reddish brown, experienced
specialists join and lay them

„Wie vernünftig ist diese
kleine handliche Form.
Welche Logik im Verband,
in Muster und Textur.
Welcher Reichtum in der
einfachen Mauerfläche!"

Ludwig Mies van der Rohe
"How reasonable is this small handy shape. What logic in the laying,
pattern and texture. What richness in the simple masonry surface!"

EMSER STRASSE,
BERLIN

Wertbeständige Schönheit:
Rund 238.000 Klinker der
dunkelrotbraunen Spezial-
sortierung „Alexander"
umhüllen die Fassaden

Beauty of lasting value:
Around 238,000 bricks of
the dark reddish-brown
special sorting "Alexander"
cover the grand facades

Ein Sinnspruch besagt: „Tradition ist nicht das Bewahren der Asche, sondern das Schüren der Flamme." Der Aphorismus des französischen Philosophen Jean Jaurès passt trefflich auf ein vertrautes, robustes Material, dessen natürliche, bei über 1000 Grad entstehende Schönheit nun wiederentdeckt wird – auch unter Nachhaltigkeitsaspekten: den Backstein, einen der ältesten Baustoffe der Welt. Seit den Hochkulturen Mesopotamiens wird die Technik des gebrannten Tons genutzt. Ging es zunächst vor allem darum, massige Mauern zu errichten, erkannten Baumeister später, dass sich mit den Kleinformaten auch kunstvolle Fassaden gestalten lassen. Selbst die Manufaktur glasierter Ziegel wurde schon in Babylon gepflegt, wovon das rekonstruierte Ischtar-Tor im Berliner Pergamonmuseum zeugt.

Von den vorderasiatischen Dynastien zieht sich eine Traditionslinie der Backstein-Architektur bis in die Gegenwart. Sie führt über die monumentalen Ziegelbauten am Forum Romanum, die nordeuropäische Backsteingotik und die Kommunalgebäude des Historismus bis zu Meisterwerken der frühen Moderne und des Expressionismus wie dem Düsseldorfer Wilhelm-Marx-Hochhaus oder dem ikonischen Chilehaus in Hamburg, beide 1924 vollendet.

An die großen Qualitäten dieser hundert Jahre alten Vorbilder knüpfen die neuen Backsteinbauten von RALF SCHMITZ an: Das zeigt sich nicht nur an der plastischen Gliederung ihrer Fassaden durch das Anordnen der Ziegel als Profile, Gesimse oder Rundbögen, sondern auch am nuancierten Farbenspiel der Backsteine. Diese stammen von Wittmunder Klinker in Ostfriesland, einer der letzten Manufakturen in Deutschland, die ihre Ziegel seit 1860 aus lokalem Ton und in traditioneller Technik ohne chemische Zusätze brennt. Anders als monotone Produkte aus industrieller Herstellung haben die Oberflächen eine unregelmäßige Textur und Färbung, weshalb Fassaden aus diesem Material so ausdrucksstark sind. „Perfekte, glatte Backsteine können wir nicht", sagt Prokurist Torsten Gilbers. „Unsere haben überbrannte Kantenabplatzer oder Trennsandrückstände – das verleiht ihnen einen ganz eigenen Charme." Im Tagesverlauf verändert sich ihr Kolorit: Im Morgenlicht dominieren kühle Töne, in der Abendsonne fangen Rottöne förmlich an zu glühen.

RALF SCHMITZ-Bauten demonstrieren, welches Spektrum der Fassadenkunst mit diesen Verblendklinkern und Formsteinen möglich ist: In Düsseldorf kleidet das Achenbach ein warmer Zinnoberton mit violetten Tupfern, in der Heinsbergstraße zeigen purpurviolett changierende Flächen weißglänzende Einsprengsel. Das Ausnahmeprojekt Alexander in Berlin prägt ein kraftvolles, dunkles Rotbraun im Spezialformat; ein Mix der lebhaften Wittmunder Klinkersortierungen 172 und 191D umhüllt das klassische Ensemble in Hamburgs Elbvorort Nienstedten.

Es sind diese handverlesenen Sortierungen der Ziegelsteine, aus denen individuelle, charaktervolle Gebäude von hoher Wertbeständigkeit entstehen, die ohne aufwendige Pflege würdig altern: Unikate, deren Schönheit besticht und höchst nachhaltig ist.

There's a saying that goes, "Tradition is not preserving the ashes, but fanning the flame." The aphorism of the French philosopher Jean Jaurès aptly fits a familiar, sturdy material whose natural beauty, created at over 1,000 degrees Celsius, is now being rediscovered – also from a sustainability perspective: brick, one of the world's oldest building materials. The technique of baked clay has been used since the advanced civilizations of Mesopotamia. Initially, it was mainly used to build solid walls, but later master builders realized that the small formats could also be used to create artistic facades. Even the manufacture of glazed bricks was practiced in Babylon, as evidenced by the reconstructed Ishtar Gate in the Pergamon Museum in Berlin.

A line of tradition in brick architecture runs from the Near Eastern dynasties to the present day. It leads via the monumental brick buildings at the Roman Forum, the Northern European brick Gothic and the diverse municipal buildings of Historicism to masterpieces of early Modernism and Expressionism, such as the Wilhelm Marx high-rise in Düsseldorf or the iconic Chilehaus in Hamburg, both completed in 1924.

RALF SCHMITZ's new brick buildings tie in with the great qualities of these hundred-year-old models: This is evident not only in the sculptural arrangement of their facades by arranging the bricks as profiles, cornices or round arches, but also in the nuanced, lively play of colors in the bricks used. These come from Wittmunder Klinker in East Frisia, the only manufactory in Germany that since 1860 to this day has been firing its bricks from local clay using traditional techniques without chemical additives. Unlike monotonous products from industrial production, the surfaces have an irregular texture and coloring, which is why facades made of them are particularly expressive. "We can't make perfect, smooth bricks," says general manager Torsten Gilbers. "Ours have overburned edge chips or separating sand residues – that gives them a charm all their own." In the course of the day, their color changes: in the morning light, cool tones dominate; in the evening sun, red tones literally begin to glow.

RALF SCHMITZ buildings demonstrate the spectrum of facade art that is possible with these clinkers and shaped bricks: In Düsseldorf, the Achenbachstraße is clothed in a warm vermilion tone with purple flecks; in the Heinsbergstraße, purple-violet iridescent surfaces display shiny white sprinkles. The exceptional project Alexander in Berlin is characterized by a powerful, dark reddish brown; a mix of grades 172 and 191D envelops the classic ensemble in Hamburg's Elbe suburb of Nienstedten.

It is the handpicked grades of the bricks from which highly individual and characterful buildings of high stable value are created, which age gracefully without costly maintenance: unique specimens made of unique bricks, whose beauty is captivating and highly sustainable.

———————

EMSER STRASSE, BERLIN

Spannungs-Bogen! Der
Rahmen für das riesige
Fensterunikat in der Pent-
house-Maisonette wurde
mittels Kran hoch hinauf ins
Staffelgeschoss gehievt

Top job! The huge arc for the
unique window in the penthouse
maisonette was lifted by
crane to the uppermost floor

FIRST-CLASS SERVICE ALL AROUND

Schönheit vereint mit höchstem Komfort – dafür sorgt bei
RALF SCHMITZ die umfassende Betreuung vom ersten Interesse an
über den individuellen Ausbau bis weit über den Einzug hinaus.

Beauty paired with the highest level of comfort – this is ensured
by the comprehensive support from the first interest
to the individualized development and far beyond the move-in date.

TEXT **Nora Scharer** FOTOS **Todd Eberle, Achim Hatzius, Gregor Hohenberg, Sebastian Treese Architekten**

Feine Vielfalt: Naturstein in
diversen Farboptionen garantiert
einen klassisch-stimmigen Look

Versatile elegance: high-quality
natural stone ensures a classically
harmonious overall design

uxus ist, genau so zu leben, wie man leben möchte. RALF SCHMITZ steht als Marke für Kompromisslosigkeit im Interesse des Kunden – ästhetisch, qualitativ und lokal verwurzelt. Zahllose zufriedene Käufer deutschlandweit hat überzeugt, was funktioniert: ein mittelständiges, familiengeführtes Unternehmen, dessen Wurzeln bis ins Jahr 1864 zurückreichen, das schnell und flexibel agiert und dem selbst gesetzten Höchstanspruch genügt, weil es mit ähnlich traditionsreichen Handwerksbetrieben sowie renommierten Architekten eng zusammenarbeitet.

Die zeitlos schöne Bauweise von RALF SCHMITZ spricht Menschen an, die den ausgesuchten Anspruch an Stilsicherheit und hochwertigste Materialien teilen. Um den Vorstellungen der künftigen Besitzer außergewöhnlichen Wohnkomforts möglichst genau entsprechen zu können, setzt das Unternehmen daher auf eine gründliche und aufmerksame Beratung. Wer sich für ein Objekt interessiert, der trifft bereits beim ersten Kontakt auf Mitarbeiter, deren Ziel nicht ein schneller Verkauf ist, sondern absolute Kundenzufriedenheit.

Selbst in den Anschauungsmaterialien, die den Interessenten dabei zur Verfügung gestellt werden, zeigen sich die Schlüsselwerte Ästhetik und Zuvorkommenheit: von der sorgfältig kuratierten Website bis hin zu den umfassenden spezifischen Informationen zu jedem neuen Projekt. Hochwertige Exposés – zeitgemäß digital, bewusst jedoch auch in erlesener Druckform haptisch erfahrbar –, und wunderschön gestaltete Grundrisse geben einen

Luxury is living exactly the way you want to live. RALF SCHMITZ as a brand stands for uncompromised devotion to the interest of the customer – both aesthetically and qualitatively. Countless satisfied buyers throughout Germany have been convinced by what works: a medium-sized and family-run company established in 1864 that remains locally rooted, flexible and quick to react, delivering on its high standards because it works only with renowned architects and skilled contractors similarly committed to traditional values.

The timelessly beautiful construction of RALF SCHMITZ appeals to people who share the select demand for style and the highest quality materials. In order to be able to correspond to the conceptions of the future owners as exactly as possible, the enterprise sets great store by a thorough and comprehensive consultation process. From the first expression of interest on, potential buyers find themselves dealing with advisers whose aim is not to conclude a quick sale, but to achieve total customer satisfaction.

Already in the visual materials provided to prospective buyers, the key values of aesthetics and courtesy are evident: from the carefully curated website to the comprehensive specific information on each new project. High-quality exposés, available both digitally and in exquisite print for a haptic experience, and beautifully designed floor plans provide a first glimpse into a new residence. Photorealistic visualizations allow the future building to be discovered in every detail. Because many of the clients know other SCHMITZ

ersten Einblick in die neue Residenz. Fotorealistische Visualisie-rungen lassen das künftige Bauwerk detailgetreu entdecken und erspüren. Weil viele der Klienten andere SCHMITZ-Immobi-lien kennen, ist das Vertrauen in neue Projekte groß. Oft werden schon in der Vorverkaufsphase alle Wohnungen erworben. Dabei wird bei der Vermittlung nichts übers Knie gebrochen: Die erfah-rene Kundenberatung hilft, eine Entscheidung zu treffen, mit der alle Beteiligten zufrieden sind. Aus diesem bewusst freundschaft-lich gestalteten Kontakt zwischen Kunde und Team entwickelt sich schließlich jenes emotionale Band, von dem eine fruchtbare Zusammenarbeit lebt.

Nach Abschluss des Kaufvertrags müssen die Kunden nichts weiter tun, als im Gespräch mit ihrem persönlichen Ansprech-partner Materialien und Produkte ihrer Innenausstattung auszu-wählen. Als bewusster Gegenpol zur üblichen Distanziertheit heutiger Kommunikation findet dieser Austausch nicht nur telefo-nisch, sondern auch persönlich in den Räumlichkeiten der jeweils zuständigen Niederlassung statt. Mit Feingefühl und Erfahrung steht die Kundenberatung bei der Bestimmung des optimalen Innern der künftigen Residenz zur Seite: Geschmackvoll abge-stimmte Kompositionen, durch Visualisierungen und Material-beispiele aus erster Hand erfahrbar, helfen bei der Auswahl des *perfect match* für die Innenausstattung – vom Ton des wertigen Eichenparketts bis hin zur edlen Armatur im Bad.

Elegante Showrooms, eingerichtet von renommierten Innende-signern wie Oliver Jungel bis hin zu Architectural Digest, lassen die

properties, confidence in new projects is high. Often, apartments are already purchased in the pre-sale phase. But nothing is rushed in this process: In keeping with the principal of customer service, experienced advisers help make the right decision. This friendly contact between the customer and the team ultimately develops the emotional bond that is the lifeblood of a fruitful collaboration.

Once the sales contract has been signed, buyers need do nothing more than select the materials and products for their desired interior with their personal adviser. As a deliberate coun-terpoint to the usual detachment of today's communication, the exchange takes place not only by telephone but also in person at the respective local SCHMITZ office. With sensitivity and experience, the customer service aids in determining the ideal interior for the future residence: tastefully coordinated composi-tions, experienced first-hand through visualizations and material examples, help in the selection of the "perfect match" for the interior – from the exact tone of the valuable oak parquet to the noble fittings in the bathroom. Elegant showrooms and show-flats, furnished by renowned interior designers ranging from Oliver Jungel to *Architectural Digest* magazine, allow customers to directly experience quality and the feeling of living, from the facade and entrance to the smallest details in the kitchen, bath-room and bedroom.

The RALF SCHMITZ team takes care of the overall imple-mentation of the selected furnishings and the intensive coordi-nation with the construction companies. In continuous contact

Linke Seite: Detaillierte Exposés
verschaffen konzise Eindrücke
eines jeden neuen Bauprojekts

Left page: Detailed materials
provide prospective
buyers with concise insights

„Man kann bei RALF SCHMITZ nur zwischen schön und schön wählen"

Eine Käuferin aus Düsseldorf
"Ultimately, with RALF SCHMITZ you can only choose between beautiful and beautiful"

Die RS-Box vereint Farbproben,
Stein- und Holzmuster passend zum
Projekt als Moodboard für Eigentümer

The RS Box combines samples for
stone, wood and color as
moodboards matching each project

Kuratierte Designlinien, ausgewählte
Bauelemente und Visualisierungen
helfen Käufern beim Entscheiden

Curated design concepts, selected
building components and visualizations
help buyers to decide themselves

„Absolut problemlos, aufmerksam,
immer lösungsorientiert,
sehr kulant und kundenfreundlich"

Ein Käufer aus Berlin
"Thoroughly uncomplicated and always friendly, focused on finding solutions,
very accommodating and customer-friendly"

Luxus erleben: Im Düsseldorfer
Showroom betreten Interessenten
Räume voller Möglichkeiten. Rechte
Seite: Ausgewählte Firmen sorgen für
den Erhalt von Ästhetik und Komfort

Diving into luxury: The showroom
in Düsseldorf provides a first glance
at how the new home could be. Right
page: Select firms ensure the
maintenance of beauty and comfort

Kunden Qualität und Wohngefühl von der Fassade übers Entree bis hin zu den kleinsten Details in der Küche, den Bädern und Schlafzimmern unmittelbar erleben.

Um die Gesamtumsetzung der gewählten Ausstattung und die intensive Abstimmung mit den am Bau beteiligten Firmen kümmert sich das RALF SCHMITZ-Team, das in fortlaufendem Kontakt zum Käufer regelmäßig zu Terminen auf die Baustelle einlädt, um Fortschritte zu besichtigen. Auch nach Schlüssel-übergabe und Einzug bleibt das Unternehmen rund um die Uhr erreichbar. „In der Gewährleistung ist guter Service besonders wichtig. Weil wir alle nur Menschen sind, kann immer mal ein Fehler passieren, den wir dann beseitigen", sagt eine Mitarbeiterin aus dem Düsseldorfer Gewährleistungsmanagement. Entsprechend positiv sind die Kundenstimmen: Umfänglicher Service und Qualitätssicherung werden zum untrennbaren Paar.

„Für uns ist der langfristige Kontakt mit den Kunden über die Herstellung der Wohnung hinaus das wichtigste und ehrlichste Feedback. Es ermöglicht uns, stetig besser zu werden, und bereitet uns die Freude, zu erleben, wie wir jemandem ein Zuhause erschaffen können", sagt Geschäftsführer Axel Martin Schmitz. Folgerichtig übernimmt sein Unternehmen auf Kundenwunsch bei Bedarf den Wiederverkauf und unterstützt auch in Renovie-rungsfragen mit großer Erfahrung und etabliertem Netzwerk. Schließlich gilt es, Schönheit zu erhalten – und so die besondere Verbindung zwischen dem traditionsreichen Bauträger und seinen hochgeschätzten Kunden nachhaltig zu pflegen.

with the buyer, the team regularly invites the client to appoint-ments at the construction site to inspect the progress. Even after handing over the keys and moving into the new home, the firm remains available around the clock. "In warranty, good service is particularly important. Because we are all only human, a mistake can always happen, which we then rectify," says an employee from the Düsseldorf warranty department. The customer testimonials are correspondingly positive: Comprehensive service and quality assurance become an inseparable pair.

"For us, long-term contact with the customers beyond the production of the apartment is the most important and honest feedback. It enables us to constantly improve and gives us the pleasure of experiencing how we can create someone's home," says Managing Director Axel Martin Schmitz. So it's only logical that, if the customer wishes so later on, the company takes on the resale and also provides support in renovation issues with an established partner network. After all, the aim is to preserve beauty – and to honor the special bond between the tradition-steeped developer and its highly valued customers in the long term.

Vom Haus aus betrachtet ist der
Garten eine Bühne, von der Straße aus
ein grüner Rahmen für die Architektur.
Für jene, die ihn nutzen, ist er ein
entspannender Mikrokosmos, in dem
es viele Welten zu entdecken gibt.

Seen from the house, the garden
is a stage; seen from the street,
it is a green frame for architecture.
For those who use it, it is a
relaxing microcosm where there
are many worlds to discover.

SERENE URBAN GREENERY

TEXT **Tanja Pabelick**

FOTOS **Iris Janke, Noshe, Heidi Scherm, Christian Stoll, Ralph Richter**

Wohnpalais Eisenzahnstraße, Berlin:
Der üppig bepflanzte Hof mit nachts
beleuchtetem Wasserspiel und großer
Loggia für alle Bewohner und Besucher

Eisenzahnstraße residential palace,
Berlin: the lushly planted courtyard
garden with a water feature that is
illuminated at night and a large loggia
for all residents and their visitors

„Der Himmel über Berlin": Von der
On-top-Terrasse des Penthouses in der
Linienstraße reicht der Blick über
große Beete weit über die Metropole

CinemaScope: From the rooftop
terrace of the Linienstraße penthouse,
fabulous views extend over large
plant beds far across the metropolis

„Ein Garten braucht Zeit, darin liegt sein Luxus"

Gabriella Pape, Königliche Gartenakademie
"A garden needs time, therein lies its luxury"

Hinter dem eleganten Kentenich Hof
liegen zwei zauberhafte Gartenvillen –
Naturrefugien inmitten der Großstadt

Behind the elegant Kentenich Hof are
two enchanting garden villas – nature
retreats in the middle of the big city

L-förmig rahmen malerische Privatgärten die gediegen-klassizistische
Doppelvilla im Berliner Grunewald

L-shaped picturesque private gardens
frame the dignified neoclassical double
villa in Berlin's Grunewald district

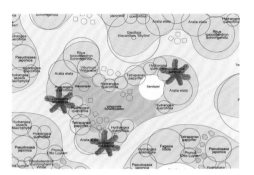

Aufwendig umgesetzt: Der Baum
wurzelt nun hinter Haus Hardt am
Johannaplatz in Grunewald. Rechts:
Hof-Planung des Projekts Alexander

Elaborately implemented: The tree
now grows behind Haus Hardt in
Berlin. On the far right: the courtyard
planning of the Alexander project

In Düsseldorf-Zoo führt eine eigene
Zufahrt durch einen großen
Privatpark zum Townhouse-Quintett

In Düsseldorf's Zoo district, a personal
driveway leads through a large
private park to the townhouse quintet

Der Schritt aus dem Zuhause in das Grün eines Gartens oder der Penthouse-Terrasse ist der Schritt in eine andere Welt. Kein Wunder, ticken die Uhren draußen doch im ganz eigenen Takt. Zwischen blühenden Stauden, wippenden Gräsern und dichten Sträuchern entsteht eine Oase der Gelassenheit und Entschleunigung, die wie eine Glocke von der urbanen Schnelllebigkeit abschirmt.

Bei jedem Vorgarten, Hof oder Freisitz hoch oben stellt sich RALF SCHMITZ die Frage nach dem individuellen Genius Loci, dem Geist des Ortes, aufs Neue. Die Architektur des Gebäudes, Lichteinfall und Lage bilden die Basis für die Inszenierung des Grüns: Mal sind es unauffällig-immergrüne Bodendecker, filigrane Farnwedel und dichte Hecken als Sichtschutz, mal gesellen sich dramatische Blattfächer zu historischem Baumbestand, mal plätschert ein Wasserspiel. Im Zusammenklang formen sich Mikrolandschaften, die von Wegen, Sitzbereichen und Sichtachsen zoniert werden. Im Frühjahr und Sommer leuchten Blüten als Farbtupfer zwischen den Blättern, anschließend prunkt der Herbst mit seinen Ocker- und Orange-Nuancen. Wer in Grünbereiche eintaucht, kann sie erforschen und immer wieder Neues finden: Hier bitten Refugien mit versteckten Bänken zur Lesepause, dort warten offenere, gemeinschaftlich genutzte Plätze auf eine zufällige Begegnung mit netten Nachbarn – und von seiner On-top-Terrasse schaut man sogar auf Landmarken der Stadt, auf deren Dachgefüge und hinauf in den Himmel. Natürlich muss bei jeder Planung auch das Praktische bedacht werden, etwa die Bewässerung und eine Wegebeleuchtung. Dazu arbeitet RALF SCHMITZ oft mit renommierten Spezialisten wie der Königlichen Gartenakademie in Berlin-Dahlem zusammen.

Deren Mitinhaberin Isabelle Van Groeningen beschreibt ihre Arbeit so: „Ich liebe es, mit Farben zu spielen, Kombinationen auszuprobieren, Farbharmonien als auch Farbkontraste passend für jede Saison zu schaffen." Ihre Grünbereiche laden Bewohner und Besucher zur stillen Betrachtung ein, immer wieder. Denn sie verändern sich im Laufe des Tages, mit der Saison und über die Jahrzehnte hinweg – blühend, wachsend und Laub abwerfend.

Ein gut gestalteter Garten bietet mit seinem wandelbaren Charakter die schönsten Blicke aus dem Fenster. Er ließe sich mit einem Orchester vergleichen, in dem nicht alle Instrumente zur gleichen Zeit spielen, das aber eine perfekt-harmonische Komposition aufführt. Seine Töne sind die Farben und die Geräusche der raschelnden Blätter, summende Bienen oder zwitschernde Vögel. Dazu kommen die Düfte: Wer wüsste nicht, wie herrlich der Frühling riecht oder feuchte Erde nach einem Sommerregen?

Begrünte Bereiche sind so viel mehr nur als nur ein Panorama, sie funktionieren als lebendige Pufferzone zur Stadt und wirken mit ihren sinnlichen Qualitäten bis in den Wohnraum hinein.

Stepping out of one's home into the green of a garden or onto the penthouse terrace is stepping into another world. No wonder, as the clocks outside are ticking at their own pace. Between flowering perennials, waving grasses and dense shrubs, an oasis of serenity and deceleration is created that shields you from the urban fast pace like a time vacuum.

With every front garden, courtyard or outdoor seating high above, RALF SCHMITZ asks himself anew the question of the individual genius loci, the special spirit of the place. The architecture of the building, the incidence of light and the location form the basis for the staging of the greenery: sometimes it is inconspicuous evergreen ground cover, filigree ferns and dense hedges as privacy screens, sometimes dramatic leaf fans join historical trees, sometimes a water feature splashes. Harmonious micro-landscapes are formed, zoned by paths, seating areas and sightlines. In spring and summer, various flowers shine as splashes of color among the leaves, then autumn flaunts its ocher and orange nuances. Those who immerse themselves in those green areas can explore them and always find something new: Here, quiet refuges with hidden benches invite you to take a reading break; there, more open, communal spaces await a chance encounter with friendly neighbors – and from a rooftop terrace, you can even look down on landmarks of the city, on its roof structure and up into the sky. Of course, practical considerations must also be taken into account in any planning, such as irrigation and path lighting. That's why RALF SCHMITZ often works with renowned specialists such as the Königliche Gartenakademie (Royal Garden Academy) in Berlin-Dahlem.

Its co-owner Isabelle Van Groeningen describes her work like this: "I love playing with colors, trying out combinations, creating color harmonies as well as color contrasts appropriate for each season." Her green spaces invite residents and visitors to quiet contemplation, again and again. Because they change throughout the day, with the season, and over the decades – blooming, growing and shedding foliage.

A well-designed garden, with its changeable character, offers the most beautiful views out the window. It could be compared to an orchestra in which not all instruments play at the same time, but which performs a perfectly-harmonious composition. Its sounds are the colors and the leaves rustling in the wind, buzzing bees or chirping birds. Then there are the scents: who wouldn't know how wonderful spring smells or damp earth after a warm summer rain?

So gardens and courtyards are much more than just a green panorama; they function as a buffer zone to the city and, with their many sensual qualities, have an effect that extends into the living space.

Im Düsseldorfer Premiumprojekt Park-terrassen schirmt der tiefe Vorgarten mit Formschnitt-Hainbuchen und Wasserspiel die 26 Wohnungen ab

In the Parkterrassen premium project in Düsseldorf, the deep front garden with hornbeam topiaries and water feature screens the 26 apartments

STRONG FAMILY TIES: A SOLID BASE

TEXT **Nora Scharer**
FOTOS **Bildarchiv der Stadt Kempen, Jakob Hermes, Gregor Hohenberg, Werner Huthmacher, Ralph Richter, Ralf Schmitz Archiv, Christian Stoll**

Baukultur seit über 160 Jahren: In Kempen am Niederrhein sind Ursprung und Fundamente des Familienunternehmens überall sichtbar.

Building culture for over 160 years: In Kempen in the Lower Rhine area, the origins and foundations of the family business are visible everywhere.

Mit zahlreichen Projekten in den Metropolen Deutschlands hat die RALF SCHMITZ GmbH sich einen Namen gemacht. Mancher mag sich da über den Stammsitz im beschaulichen Kempen wundern. Ein solches Unternehmen und eine kleine Stadt am Niederrhein – wie passt das zusammen? Axel Martin Schmitz, geschäftsführender Gesellschafter und Vertreter der fünften Generation des Familienunternehmens, bringt es auf den Punkt: „Ich wüsste nicht, wie man mehr mit einem Städtchen verbunden sein kann." Denn ein Blick auf die Unternehmenshistorie zeigt: Die Geschichte des Ortes und der Familie sind aufs Engste verwoben. Das prägt.

Beginnend mit der Gründung der Kempener Niederlassung 1906 durch Heinrich Schmitz sind Familie und Bauunternehmen fest in der Stadt verwurzelt. Im Ort und um ihn herum entstehen zahlreiche Klöster, Kirchen, Fabriken und Wohnhäuser. Die vierte und fünfte Generation der Familie wurde im vom Vorfahren erbauten Krankenhaus in Kempen geboren, im Hospital zum Heiligen Geist. Wie schon ihr Vater besuchten auch Axel Martin Schmitz und seine Brüder das Gymnasium Thomaeum (vom Urgroßvater errichtet als Königliches Lehrerseminar).

Als Ralf Schmitz mit Gründung seiner eigenen Wohnungsbaugesellschaft 1977 die ersten Immobilien in Kempen erwirbt,

RALF SCHMITZ GmbH has made a name for itself with countless projects in Germany's major cities. Some may wonder about the company's headquarters in the tranquil town of Kempen. Such a company and a small town on the Lower Rhine – how does that fit together? Axel Martin Schmitz, managing partner and representative of the fifth generation of the family business, puts it in a nutshell: "I don't know how you can be more connected to a small town." Because a look at the company history shows: The history of the town and the family are closely interwoven. That leaves its mark.

Starting with the founding of the Kempen branch in 1906 by Heinrich Schmitz, the family and the construction company are firmly rooted in the town. Numerous monasteries, churches, factories and residential buildings were built in and around the town. The fourth and fifth generations of the family were born in the hospital built by their ancestor in Kempen, the Hospital zum Heiligen Geist. Like their father, Axel Martin Schmitz and his brothers also attended the Thomaeum grammar school (built by their great-grandfather as a royal teachers' seminary with a Neo-baroque bell tower).

When Ralf Schmitz founded his own company in 1977 and bought his first properties in Kempen, one of them was the house

Ralf Schmitz im Archivraum des
Kempener Stammsitzes vor Porträts
seiner Vorfahren im Familienunternehmen

Ralf Schmitz in the archive room of the
Kempen headquarters in front of portraits
of his ancestors in the family business

ist darunter auch das Haus, in dem seine Kinder groß werden – nach eigenhändiger Renovierung des baufälligen Gebäudes unter den strengen Augen des Vaters Hieronymus. Lächelnd erzählt Axel Martin Schmitz von seinem ersten Nebenjob noch zu Schulzeiten: Platzanweiser im Lichtspielhaus Kempen, 1913 von seinem Urgroßvater mitbegründet und errichtet.

Ob sie jedes von einem Vorfahren erbaute Gebäude kennen? Ralf Schmitz nickt: „Was in Kempen aus Schmitz'schen Händen gebaut ist, das erkenne ich schon. Hier und in der Umgebung gibt

in which his children grew up – after renovating the dilapidated building himself under the strict eyes of his father Hieronymus. Axel Martin Schmitz smiles as he tells of his first part-time job when he was still at school: usher at the Kempen cinema, co-founded and built by his great-grandfather in 1913.

Do they know every building built by an ancestor? Ralf Schmitz nods: "I do recognize what was constructed in Kempen by Schmitz hands. Here and in the surrounding area are really many formative and significant buildings that our family created." His son agrees: "I've experienced it since I was a child: When you walk through the streets here, for quite a lot of the houses there is a story about who in the family had built it or renovated something there. With that comes a certain pride – but above all the responsibility to carry on this heritage properly."

At the company's headquarters Villa Brandenburg, the connection with the city's history is particularly palpable. Acquired by Ralf Schmitz in 1998 in need of rehabilitation and renovated from the ground up, the listed building shows that love of detail, that combination of timeless aesthetics and comfort that always characterizes the buildings of the family business. From the uppermost window under the roof gable, one looks east towards a Kempen landmark: the water tower – built by the family in 1905/06.

Nachdem 2014 der erste Entwurf des
Baus an der Stadtmauer für Kritik
gesorgt hatte, fand Axel Martin Schmitz
im offenen Gespräch, unter anderem
mit dem Kempener Historiker Hans
Kaiser, eine konstruktive Lösung für
den Erhalt der historisch wertvollen
Fassade des alten Gebäudes an
der Peterstraße

After the first draft for the building
on the city wall was criticized in 2014,
Axel Martin Schmitz found a con-
structive solution to preserve the
historically valuable facade of the
old building on Peterstraße in an
open discussion with historian
Hans Kaiser and others

Fabrikgebäude Johannes Girmes & Co.,
Grefrath-Oedt (1883–1886)

Kinematographentheater
Buttermarkt (1913)

Hospital zum Heiligen Geist
(1914–1917)

„Wenn ich durch Kempen
gehe, gibt es zu fast jedem
Haus eine Geschichte,
welcher Vorfahr es gebaut
oder saniert hatte"

Axel Martin Schmitz
"When I walk through Kempen, almost every house has a story
about which ancestor built or renovated it"

Grachtenpark (2006–2013)

Königliches Lehrerseminar
(1909/10) / Gymnasium Thomaeum

es wirklich viele prägende und bedeutende Bauten, die unsere Familie errichtet hat." Sein Sohn pflichtet ihm bei: „Ich kenne das schon von Kind auf: Wenn man hier durch die Straßen ging, gab es zu fast jedem Haus eine Geschichte, wer in der Familie es gebaut oder dort etwas saniert hatte. Damit geht ein gewisser Stolz einher – vor allem aber die Verantwortung, dieses Erbe gebührend fortzuführen."

Im Stammsitz des Unternehmens, der Villa Brandenburg, spürt man die Verbindung mit der Geschichte der Stadt besonders. 1998 in sanierungsbedürftigem Zustand von Ralf Schmitz erworben und von Grund auf renoviert, zeigt das Baudenkmal jene Liebe zum Detail, jene Verbindung von zeitloser Ästhetik und nachhal-

„Wir sind der traditionellen Architektur bis heute verpflichtet geblieben"

Ralf Schmitz
"We have remained committed to traditional architecture to this day"

tigem Komfort, die die Bauwerke des Familienunternehmens stets charakterisiert. Aus dem obersten Fenster unterm Dachgiebel blickt man gen Osten auf ein Kempener Wahrzeichen: den Wasserturm – 1905/06 von der Familie errichtet.

Vier Etagen tiefer, vorbei an detaillierten Modellen wegweisender Projekte der letzten Jahrzehnte, an Reihen von Ordnern und zahllosen Unterlagen, findet sich im Souterrain das Herzstück des Hauses: Gemälde und Fotografien der Ahnen zieren einen Raum, in dem Historie erfahrbar wird. Auf dem großen Tisch in der Mitte liegen die letzten Mappen voll mit Fotografien, Dokumenten und Zeitungsartikeln über die Geschichte der Familie Schmitz zur Etikettierung und Sortierung. Ehrenamtlich, im Gegenzug für Spenden an ein Kameruner Waisenhaus, führte der renommierte Kempener Historiker Dr. Hans Kaiser diese Archivarbeit durch. Ergänzend zur Chronik von Prof. Wolfgang Schäche „Architektur und Handwerk. Bauten der Unternehmerfamilie Schmitz 1864–2014" sortierte Kaiser das nun 700 Mappen füllende Archiv, recherchierte nach. In staubfreien Kartons verwahrt, akribisch beschriftet und katalogisiert, ist es jetzt für die Zukunft aufbereitet.

„Mir war es wichtig, die umfangreiche Geschichte unserer Familie auch für kommende Generationen fassbar zu bewahren", so Ralf Schmitz. Schließlich bildet das Archiv eine hochpersönliche Grundlage zum architektonischen Werk des Bauunternehmens. Es ist Sinnbild für eine Familie, deren sorgfältige Handschrift jedes ihrer Gebäude prägt – ein immenser Reichtum, der in fast 160 Jahren realisiert wurde. Diese Verantwortung ruft sich die Familie bei jedem Gang durch die Heimat bewusst in Erinnerung, wie Axel Martin Schmitz verdeutlicht: „Wir haben das große Glück, dass wir am Kempener Stadbild seit mehreren Generationen mitwirken dürfen. Ich hoffe, dass auch spätere Generationen gutheißen, was wir hier geschaffen haben – und was wir in die Metropolen des Landes getragen haben und weiter tragen werden."

Four floors below, past detailed models of pioneering projects of prior decades, rows of folders and countless documents, the heart of the house is found in the basement: paintings and photographs of the ancestors adorn a room in which history can be experienced. On the large table in the middle, the last folders full of photographs, documents and newspaper articles about the history of the Schmitz family await being labelled and sorted. On a voluntary basis, in exchange for donations to a Cameroonian orphanage, the renowned Kempen historian Dr. Hans Kaiser carried out this archival work. Complementing the chronicle by Prof. Wolfgang Schäche "Architecture and Craftsmanship; Buildings of the Schmitz Family 1864-2014," Kaiser sorted through the archive, which today fills 700 folders, and added to the research. Stored in dust-free boxes, meticulously labelled and catalogued, it is now prepared for the future.

"It was important to me to tangibly preserve the extensive history of our family for future generations," says Ralf Schmitz. After all, the archive forms a highly personal basis for the architectural work of the construction company. It is a symbol of a family whose meticulous handwriting characterizes each of its buildings – an immense wealth that has been realized over 160 years. The family consciously recalls this responsibility every time they walk through their native city, as Axel Martin Schmitz makes clear: "We are very fortunate to have been able to contribute

a great deal to Kempen's townscape over several generations. I hope that later generations will also approve of what we have created here – and what we have carried into and will continue to carry into the metropolises of the country."

Der Klosterhof, eines der bedeutendsten Projekte jüngerer Zeit im Herzen der Altstadt, wurde im Vorfeld öffentlich heiß diskutiert. Mit der Eröffnung 2014 wich die Anfangsskepsis breiter Begeisterung. Links: Die denkmalgeschützte Villa Brandenburg, Stammsitz des Unternehmens seit 1998. Linke Seite: Der Kempener Wasserturm, erbaut 1905/06

The Klosterhof in the heart of the old town, one of Kempen's most important recent projects, was hotly debated in public in the run-up. With the opening in 2014, skepticism gave way to enthusiasm. Left, the listed Villa Brandenburg, the company's headquarters since 1998. Left page: the Kempen water tower, built in 1905/06 by an ancestor

GLAMOROUS
DRESSING ROOMS

Auf Kundenwunsch maßgefertigte Ankleiden schaffen Ordnung, sind intimer Rückzugsort und Schleuse zwischen Schlaf- und Badezimmer.

Dressing rooms made to measure upon buyers' wishes create order, are an intimate retreat and a port between bedroom and bathroom.

TEXT **Florian Siebeck** FOTOS **Todd Eberle, Gregor Hohenberg, Noshe, Pure, Ralph Richter**

Greifweg, Düsseldorf: Gebürstete Eiche, grau gebeizt und lackiert, prägt diese reduziert-elegante Ankleide. Die Türgriffe sind eine Sonderanfertigung; alle Schübe öffnen sich per Antippen

Greifweg, Düsseldorf: Brushed oak, stained and lacquered gray, characterizes this elegant dressing room. The door handles are custom-made; all drawers open via push-on system

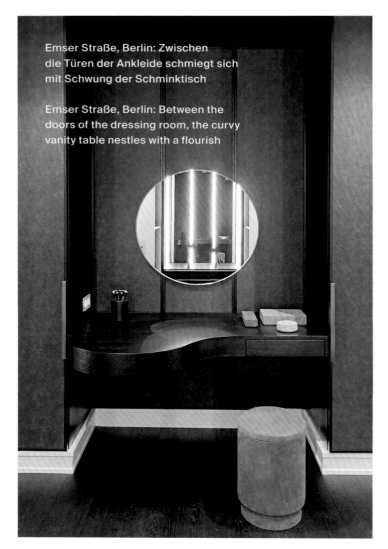

Emser Straße, Berlin: Zwischen
die Türen der Ankleide schmiegt sich
mit Schwung der Schminktisch

Emser Straße, Berlin: Between the
doors of the dressing room, the curvy
vanity table nestles with a flourish

Degerstraße, Düsseldorf: Die Profile
der lichten Ankleide sind denen
der Zimmertüren nachempfunden

Degerstraße, Düsseldorf: The
profiles of this dressing room mimic
those of the apartment's doors

Wer einen begehbaren Kleiderschrank hat, erntet dafür manchmal süffisante Blicke. Dabei unterschätzen Spötter, dass ein Ankleidezimmer weit mehr ist als eine Art persönlicher Boutique. Wer einmal den Luxus eines aufgeräumten Schlafzimmers ganz ohne Schränke (oder gar Schmutzwäschekörbe!) erfahren hat, der wird nur schwer auf eine Ankleide verzichten können, ob sie nun einen Kleiderlift oder ein Belüftungssystem hat oder nicht. Die Ankleide ist wie die Vorratskammer einer Küche: Sie dient dem größeren Raum und hält ihn für das Wesentliche frei. Ganz ohne wuchtige Kleiderschränke lässt es sich auch viel befreiter schlafen. Deswegen gilt gerade in guten Wohnlagen eine Ankleide als der ultimative und zugleich praktische Luxus.

Als Schleuse zwischen Schlaf- und Badezimmer erfüllt die Ankleide zudem eine wichtige Funktion: Sie wird zum Rückzugsort für private Stunden, fast wie ein spezielles Wohnzimmer. Ein Raum für Schönheitsrituale, auch unabhängig vom Partner. Und da sind wir noch nicht mal bei der Außenwirkung: Durch die übersichtliche Aufteilung der (faltenfreien!) Kleidungsstücke lässt sich das Outfit morgens viel leichter zusammenstellen; ein Pluspunkt in unserer visuell geprägten Gesellschaft. Alte Kleidung kann schnell identifiziert und aussortiert werden. Und falls doch mal was liegen bleibt, fällt es nicht gleich ins Auge – anders als im Schlafzimmer, wo oft ein Stuhl als Notlösung für halb getragene Wäsche herhalten muss.

Anyone who has a walk-in closet sometimes earns smug looks for it. But scoffers underestimate that a dressing room is much more than a kind of personal boutique. Anyone who has experienced the luxury of a tidy bedroom without any closets (or even dirty laundry baskets!) will find it hard to do without a dressing room. Whether it needs a clothes lift or a ventilation system is another matter. Rather, it is like the pantry of a kitchen: it serves the larger space and keeps it free for the essentials. Without bulky closets, it is also possible to sleep much more freely. That's why, especially in good residential areas, a dressing room is considered the ultimate and at the same time practical luxury.

As a gateway between the bedroom and bathroom, the dressing room also fulfills an important function: it becomes a retreat for private hours, almost like a special living room. A space for beauty rituals, independent of the partner. And we're not even talking about the external effect: the clear arrangement of the (wrinkle-free!) garments makes it much easier to combine outfits in the morning; a plus point in our visually-driven society. Outdated clothes can be quickly identified and sorted out. And if something does get left behind, it's not so obvious – unlike in the bedroom, where a chair is often used as a makeshift solution for half-worn laundry.

Dressing rooms – or glam rooms, as they have recently been renamed – used to be called boudoirs: small, intimate, elegant rooms

Goldfinkweg, Berlin: Das Licht in
den deckenhohen Schränken geht
an, wenn man die Türen öffnet;
eine Bank erleichtert das Anziehen

Goldfinkweg, Berlin: Inside the ceiling-
high cabinets, lighting comes on
as soon as you open the doors. The
bench facilitates putting on shoes

Eisenzahnstraße, Berlin: Ein Boudoir, modern interpretiert. Hölzer, ein kluges Lichtkonzept und der Teppich verleihen dem großzügigen Bereich zwischen Bad und Schlafraum Wärme

Eisenzahnstraße, Berlin: a boudoir, interpreted in a modern way. Woods, a clever lighting concept and the carpet give warmth to the spacious area between bath and bedroom

Als Schleuse zwischen Schlaf- und Badezimmer erfüllt die Ankleide eine weitere wichtige Funktion

As a lock between the bedroom and the bathroom, the dressing room fulfills another important function

Zwei Stauraumwunder: weiß lackiert
mit hohem Schuhauszug und Sitzbank,
aus Eiche im Stil japanischer Tempel

Two storage wonders: white lacquered
with tall shoe pull-out and seat,
oak in the style of Japanese temples

Ankleidezimmer – oder *glam rooms,* wie sie neuerdings genannt werden – hießen früher noch Boudoir: ein kleiner, intim-eleganter Raum mit viel Samt und schweren Stoffen, in den sich die Dame des Hauses zurückziehen konnte. Mit Frisiertisch, Schminkspiegel, Sitzbank, manchmal gar mit einer Badewanne. Auch die Herren hatten eigene Ankleide-, Frisier- und Rasierzimmer. Diese Räume waren äußerst wichtig, denn bevor es Badezimmer gab, fand die gesamte Morgentoilette in der Ankleide statt. Boudoirs inspirierten Kunst und Literatur, etwa „La Philosophie dans le boudoir" von Marquis de Sade oder die gesellschaftskritischen Boudoirszenen von William Hogarth.

In der 1864 erschienenen Romanserie „Can You Forgive Her?" beschreibt Anthony Trollope das Ankleidezimmer seiner Lady Glencora, das „mit den bequemsten Stühlen, den kostbarsten Schränken und den wunderlichsten Porzellanornamenten" ausgestaltet ist. „Ich nenne es mein Ankleidezimmer", sagt die reiche Erbin, „weil ich auf diese Weise die Leute davon fernhalten kann." Damals recht ungewöhnlich – denn etwa in Frankreich war es zu jener Zeit gang und gäbe, auch Gäste in der Ankleide zu unterhalten; es gab genügend Fauteuils und Liegen, um enge Freunde ebenso wie Geschäftspartner zu empfangen.

Nach all den Retrowellen im Wohnbereich ist dies vielleicht das nächste große Comeback …?

with lots of velvet and heavy fabrics, where the lady of the house could retreat. With a dressing table, make-up mirror, bench, sometimes even a bathtub. The gentlemen also had their own dressing, hairdressing and shaving rooms. These rooms were extremely important, because before there were bathrooms, all the morning toilette took place in the dressing room. Boudoirs inspired literature and art, such as *La Philosophie dans le boudoir* by Marquis de Sade and the socially critical boudoir scenes by William Hogarth.

In *Can You Forgive Her?,* a series of novels published in 1864, Anthony Trollope describes his Lady Glencora's dressing room, which is furnished with "the most comfortable chairs, the most costly cupboards, and the quaintest china ornaments." "I call it my dressing room," said the wealthy heiress, "because that way I can keep people out of it." Quite unusual at the time – because in France, for example, it was then commonplace to entertain guests in the dressing room as well; there were enough easy chairs and couches to accommodate close friends or business associates.

After all the retro waves in the living area, perhaps this is the next big comeback …?

PREUSSENALLEE, BERLIN WESTEND

Ein elegantes Dach aus dunklem Schiefer,
typisch für dieses gediegene Villenviertel,
krönt den lichten Bau mit vier Wohnungen
auf dem 1400 qm großen Eckgrundstück

An elegant dark slate mansard roof, typical
of this dignified villa district, crowns the
luminous building with four units on
an approximately 1,400 sqm corner plot

OUTSTANDING APARTMENT HOUSES

TEXT **Ina Marie Kühnast**

FOTOS **Gregor Hohenberg, Katja Hiendlmayer, Werner Huthmacher, Noshe, Ralph Richter, Christian Stoll, Sebastian Treese Architekten**

Stadtvillen von RALF SCHMITZ vereinen zeitlose und schöne Architekturen mit dem Komfort und der Technik von heute.

These handsome properties combine classically styled architecture with the luxuries and amenities of today.

AM SCHÜLERHEIM, BERLIN DAHLEM

Landhaus-Look 2.0: Der Glanz der Grün-
derzeit stand Pate für dieses schneeweiße
Gebäude mit feinen Putzprofilen und
klassischen Sprossenfenstern. Rechts:
Eingang zu drei der Einheiten, die vierte
Wohnung hat einen separaten Zugang

Country house, reimagined: Turn-of-the-
century splendor inspired this snow-white
building with delicate plaster profiles and
classic mullioned windows. On the right:
The entry to three of the units, the fourth
apartment has its own separate entrance

LINIENSTRASSE, BERLIN MITTE

Nobler Minimalismus im Herzen der
Hauptstadt: Hinter der Kalksteinfassade
liegen sieben loftartige Wohnungen

Noble minimalism at the very heart
of the capital: Seven loft-style apartments
are behind the limestone facade

TIERGARTENSTRASSE,
DÜSSELDORF DÜSSELTAL

Zahlreiche Gauben im Walmdach,
dominante Loggien und betonte Gesimse
verleihen Haus Hardenberg mit seinen
sechs Domizilen Anmut und Imposanz

Numerous dormers in the hip roof,
imposing loggias and accentuated
cornices lend Hardenberg House with
six domiciles its commanding grace

BILKER STRASSE,
DÜSSELDORF CARLSTADT

Als hätte es schon immer hier gestanden:
Diskret fügt sich das historisch anmutende
Gebäude mit fünf Geschossen ein;
zusammen mit dem Hofhaus bietet
es rund 1900 qm Wohnfläche

As if it always stood here: The historic-
looking building with five stories
blends in discreetly; it and the lower
brick-clad courtyard house offer around
1,900 sqm of elegant living space

DEGERSTRASSE,
DÜSSELDORF FLINGERN/NORD

Elf Apartments im Kreativviertel: Schlanke
Fenster gliedern die klassizistische
Fassade, moosgrüne Klinkerriemchen
schmücken die zwei unteren Etagen

Eleven apartments in the creative quarter:
sleek windows structure the neoclassical
facade, moss-green clinker brick
bands adorn the two lower floors

SALIERSTRASSE,
DÜSSELDORF OBERKASSEL

Elegant schwingt sich das schmucke
Gebäude um die Straßenecke und macht
bereits aus der Ferne durch die auf-
gesetzte Rotunde auf sich aufmerksam

This handsome building elegantly follows
the street corner's curve and its gorgeous
rooftop rotunda catches the eye from afar

Ein Deutscher revolutionierte einst den New Yorker *way of living:* George Henry Griebel entwarf das legendäre The Dakota, das 1884 am Central Park entstand. Seine Idee, 65 Luxuswohnungen mit bis zu zwanzig Zimmern in einem einzigen Gebäude zu vereinen, galt als epochal. Denn bis dato lebten vermögende Familien stets in freistehenden Villen auf großen Grundstücken außerhalb, im turbulenten Zentrum wohnten eher ärmere Bevölkerungsschichten in Mehrfamilienhäusern. Groß war die Entrüstung der New Yorker, dass Familien der *upper class* komfortabel unter einem Dach leben sollten. Man tuschelte, was in diesem Domizil so alles vor sich gehen würde …

Noch viel mehr Aufgebrachtheiten bekam Georges-Eugène Haussmann, Präfekt von Paris unter Napoleon III., zu hören, als er ab 1853 mit der radikalen Neuanlage der Seine-Metropole begann. Die Pariser hingen sehr an ihren schmalen, nur selten vielstöckigen Häusern, die die engen Gassen der Innenstadt säumten. Im Erdgeschoss lag meist ein Geschäft, die Wohnung des Ladeninhabers direkt darüber. In den übrigen *appartements* lebte die Arbeiterklasse; der Bevölkerungszunahme geschuldet, vermietete man sogar Dachkammern als kostengünstige Studios. Von Pariser Großbürgertum also – noch – keine Spur. Im neuen Zentrum à la Haussmann wurden dann die Fronten breiter, die Fassaden höher und klassizistisch-homogener und Straßen wie die Rue de Rivoli zum Vorbild für prächtige Boulevards, die bis heute Paris prägen. Das Interesse von Haussmann galt dem Gesamtensemble, er vereinheitlichte Material, Dimensionen und bestimmte wiederkehrende Fassadenelemente. Die mittelalterliche Enge wich lichten Alleen von eleganten Häusern, einem baulichen Spiegelbild der aufkommenden bürgerlichen Gesellschaft.

Der Exkurs in die Geschichte zeigt, wo die schmucken Stadtvillen wie Eisenzahn 1 in Berlin, der Greifweg oder das Deger's in Düsseldorf ihre Wurzeln haben. Mehrfamilienhäuser von RALF SCHMITZ setzen auf jenen bis heute anziehend wirkenden traditionellen Charme und zitieren vom Klassizismus bis zur Art déco die Architekturgeschichte. An den eleganten, weltstädtisch anmutenden Fassaden lässt sich die außergewöhnlich hohe bauliche Qualität ablesen. Zugleich passen diese Stadtvillen sich kompromisslos dem zeitgenössischen Lebensstil und Komfort an, ohne modernistischen Trends zu erliegen.

Jedes neu errichtete SCHMITZ-Haus regt die Fantasie aller an, die es betrachten: Wie wohnt es sich wohl auf der Beletage dieses Dahlem-Juwels, welche Epoche inspirierte zu der geschwungenen Fassade der Salierstraße, wie blau schimmert der See von den Terrassen der Trabener Straße aus? Die fein abgestimmten Gesamtkunstwerke aus Bau, Umgebung und Ausstattung versprühen die Magie ihrer architektonischen Vorbilder entlang berühmter Avenues und Boulevards dieser Welt und spannen einen stilistischen Bogen in die Gegenwart.

In 1884, a German revolutionized New York living. With his design for the now legendary Dakota building on Central Park West, George Henry Griebel set out to combine 65 luxury apartments with up to 20 rooms each under one roof – a then unprecedented idea. Wealthy families had hitherto lived in free-standing villas built on large plots out of town, while apartment blocks in the city's center were the preserve of the less fortunate. To many New Yorkers, the idea that multiple well-to-do families should live happily in the same building was scandalous, and there was much gossiping about what these occupants might get up to …

An den eleganten Fassaden lässt sich die außergewöhnliche Bauqualität ablesen

Their timelessly elegant facades transmit exceptional standards of construction quality

Even greater opprobrium greeted Georges-Eugène Haussmann, prefect of Paris under Napoleon III, when he began his radical reorganization of the French capital in 1853. People were very fond of the narrow, mostly low-built houses that lined the crowded streets of central Paris. Their ground floors generally contained retail premises, with the shopkeeper living directly above and the remaining flats being occupied by members of the working class. After Haussmann, all that changed. His remodelled city center featured wider, higher frontages that were more homogenous and classical in style, with roads such as Rue de Rivoli providing the template for the grand boulevards typical of modern-day Paris.

This historical digression outlines where the roots of properties such as Berlin's Eisenzahn 1 or Düsseldorf's Greifweg and Deger's lie. The undimmed appeal of the Dakota and of Haussmann's Paris is, after all, one that continues to inform the architecture of our buildings, which draw on traditions from Neoclassicism to Art Deco. From the outside, their timeless facades speak of exceptional standards of build quality, while inside, their living spaces are perfectly tailored to today's lifestyles yet steer clear of short-lived trends. Every new RALF SCHMITZ development fires the imagination and inspires the curiosity of passers-by.

Carefully combining exterior, interior and environment, these aesthetically pleasing properties capture the magic their architectural forebears brought to world-famous avenues and boulevards – and transpose it to the present day.

BROHLER STRASSE, KÖLN MARIENBURG

Das erste Projekt von RALF SCHMITZ
in Köln! Der lichte Bau mit klassischem
Bossen- und Kammputz soll sechs
Wohnungen umfassen; zwei davon mit
Privatgärten. Heutigen Komfort bieten der
elegante Lift, eine Tiefgarage mit elf
Stellplätzen plus Fahrradraum und eine
moderne Wärmepumpe. Die stille Straße
mit ihrer prächtigen Mittelallee aus
Platanen ist Garant für gehobenes Wohnen

The first project by RALF SCHMITZ in
Cologne! The luminous building with
classic ashlar and crested plaster will offer
six apartments, two of them with private
gardens. Modern comfort is provided by
an elevator, an underground garage with
eleven parking spaces plus a bicycle room
and a modern heat pump. The quiet street
with its magnificent central plane tree
avenue is a guarantee for upscale living

TRABENER STRASSE, BERLIN HALENSEE

Die Duplex-Wohnungen bieten
zusätzliche Wohnräume auf der
Gartenebene. Grauer Kalkstein rahmt
die Wasserspiele auf den Terrassen

The two duplexes offer additional living
space at the garden level. Gray limestone
frames the water features on the terraces

GREIFWEG, DÜSSELDORF OBERKASSEL

Die luxuriöse Mittelfassade des neuen Trios
ist aus Vert de Salvan, einem Schweizer
Naturstein; es entstanden 16 Wohnungen

The luxurious central facade of the trio is
made of Vert de Salvan, a Swiss natural
stone; 16 apartments were created in total

EISENZAHNSTRASSE,
BERLIN CHARLOTTENBURG

Exquisites Stadtpalais beim Kurfürstendamm mit zwölf Domizilen: Starke
horizontale Balustradenlinien und die
sanft gekurvten Risalite spielen mit
klassischem Formenvokabular à la Paris

Exquisite residence near the Kurfürstendamm with twelve domiciles: strong
horizontal lines of the balustrades and
the gently curved avant-corps play with
a classical Parisian vocabulary of forms

**CHARLOTTE-NIESE-STRASSE,
HAMBURG NIENSTEDTEN**

Familienleben im schönsten Elbvorort:
Mattroter Klinker und Mansarddächer
zitieren typisch hanseatische Architektur

Family life in the most beautiful Elbe
suburb: matte red bricks and mansard
roofs cite typical Hanseatic architecture

ATTENTION TO DETAILS

TEXT **Bettina Schneuer**

FOTOS **Gregor Hohenberg, Werner Huthmacher, Stefan Müller, Noshe, Ralph Richter, Sebastian Treese Architekten, Tania Walck**

Baby, Light My Wire! „Circuit",
Glaskapseln in Messinghüllen
von der New Yorker Manufaktur
Apparatus, leuchten im Foyer
der Berliner Linienstraße,
deren Treppenhaus (linke Seite)
ein minimalistisches Farbkonzept
prägt: Freiwangen aus schwarzem
Metall, Stufen und Boden aus
Silver Travertine-Naturstein

Baby, Light My Wire! "Circuit",
glass capsules in brass cases by
New York-based manufacturer
Apparatus, light up the lobby of
Berlin's Linienstraße, whose
stairwell (left side) is characterized
by a minimalist color concept:
Plate stringers made of black
metal, steps and floor of
Silver Travertine natural stone

Die große Kraft der kleinen Dinge: Hochwertige
Bauelemente und feine Manufakturakzente
charakterisieren alle RALF SCHMITZ-Gebäude.

The great strength of small things:
High-quality building elements and refined manufactory
accents characterize all RALF SCHMITZ projects.

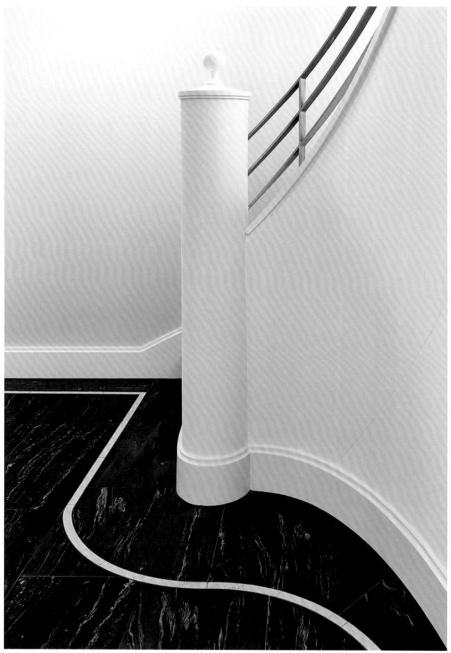

Typische SCHMITZ-Details:
Böden aus zeitlosem Naturstein;
Türdrücker aus Bisschops klassischer
„Bauhaus"-Serie; stilvolle
Türolive in brüniertem Messing

Typical SCHMITZ details: Floors
made of fine natural stone;
door handles from Bisschop's
classic "Bauhaus" series; stylish
door olive in burnished brass

Fein profilierte Türen, haptisch schöne Griffe und kunstvoll verlegter Naturstein adeln die Häuser

Finely profiled doors, haptically beautiful handles and
artfully laid natural stone ennoble the houses

Prägnant an der Wand: Den Pietra-
Grigia-Foyerbrunnen, ein Unikat,
entwarf das Studio Oliver Jungel

The Pietra Grigia foyer fountain,
a unique piece, was made after
a design by studio Oliver Jungel

GARTEN

SIGMARINGER STRASSE 17a

Zwölf Briefkästen aus patiniertem Messing, gerahmt mit warm-tonigem Kirschholz, bilden einen markanten Akzent im Eingang der Sigmaringer Straße, Berlin

Twelve mailboxes made of patinated brass, framed with warm cherrywood, form a striking accent in the foyer of the building on Sigmaringer Straße, Berlin

Auch Elemente für alle Bewohner, etwa die Briefkastenanlagen, sind gekonnt komponiert

Elements for all residents, such as the mailboxes, are masterfully composed as well

Beide Eingangsloggien des U-förmigen Düsseldorfer Ensembles zieren großformatige Edelstahl-Unterputzanlagen

Large recessed letterboxes in stainless steel adorn both entrance porches at this U-shaped ensemble in Düsseldorf

Düsseldorf, Achenbachstraße: In den beiden Foyers wurde Baubronze mit dunklem Holz kombiniert. Die aufwendig in die Wand eingepasste neue Anlage wird mit der Zeit wunderschöne Patina ansetzen

Düsseldorf, Achenbachstraße: Architectural bronze was combined with dark wood in the two foyers. The new system, which was elaborately fitted into the wall, will acquire a beautiful patina over time

Moosgrün lasierte Klinkerriemchen
an der Fassade finden ihr Pendant
im Treppenhaus der Degerstraße,
Düsseldorf. Die wellenförmige Front
des Kentenich Hofs im Stil des
Art déco setzt sich im Innerem fort –
die Elemente des Treppenhauses
tragen zeitloses Schwarz-Weiß

Moss green glazed clinker bricks
on the facade find their pendant in the
stairwell of Degerstraße, Düsseldorf.
The undulating exterior of Kentenich
Hof with nods to Art Deco is continued
inside – the staircase's elements
wear timeless black and white

Daniel Miller, Anthropologie-Professor am renommierten University College London, beschäftigt sich mit der sogenannten materiellen oder materialen Kultur, also mit der Frage, wie sich Persönlichkeit und Lebensverhältnisse eines Menschen in jenen Objekten widerspiegeln, mit denen er sich in seinen vier Wänden umgibt: von Urgroßmutters Goldrandgeschirr über neue, edle Sonus-faber-Lautsprecher oder einen sternekochwürdigen Herd von Molteni bis zur verschrammten Holzkommode aus Kindertagen – tröstlich, speziell oder erinnerungsgeladen, immer aber: emotional wichtig.

Diese Alltagsforschung über die Dingbedeutsamkeit im eigenen Zuhause lässt sich auch übertragen auf es selbst: Wie muss eine Wohnung beschaffen sein, um sich darin dauerhaft wohlzufühlen? Was macht das sie umgebende Haus zum Kontrapunkt des unruhigen Draußen? Bei RALF SCHMITZ setzt man dafür auf eine Selektion des bewährt Schönen aus anderen Epochen, auf Bauelemente, die seit jeher für Großzügigkeit, Eleganz und Stil stehen. Umgesetzt von Handwerksbetrieben, die, ob Stuckateure, Steinmetze, Schlosser, Parkettleger, Fenster- oder Treppenbauer, allesamt wahre Meister ihres Faches sind und noch tradierte Künste beherrschen.

Handfest einerseits – hochemotional andererseits: Denn die weiche Rundung eines geschmiedeten Türknaufs erfreut jedes Mal den, der ihn berührt. Minimal unregelmäßige Natursteinfliesen im Bad erden nicht nur nackte Füße, sie sind nahezu ewig haltbar und zeitlos schön. Das Klacken von Absätzen auf elegantem Eichenparkett kündigt die Liebste an, auf die man gewartet hat.

„Stuck ist alter Glanz und traditionelles Handwerk, kein Luxus", sagt Ulrich Jacobi dazu. Seit über 30 Jahren arbeiten der Meister und seine rund 20 Mitarbeiter daran, historische Bauten wieder schön zu machen – und neue Gebäude prächtiger. Für das SCHMITZ-Haus an der Eisenzahnstraße lieferte er über 1000 Meter handgefertigte Stuckleisten; die dafür eigens gebauten Schablonen aus Holz und Blech umfassten knapp 15 verschiedene, von Architekt Sebastian Treese entwickelte Motivformen.

Das Besondere, ästhetisch Herausragende setzt sich fort in den allen zugänglichen Bereichen eines jeden SCHMITZ-Hauses: Einer von dunklem Holz markant umrahmten Briefkasten-anlage aus patiniertem Messing entnimmt man sogar Post vom Finanzamt zur Körperschaftsteuererklärung mit Anlage OG gern (nahezu jedenfalls). Passend zum exotischen Flair des neuen Apartmenthauses Emser Straße setzte Gestalter Oliver Jungel für die Treppenhäuser auf Berker-Schalter in einem speziellen Messing mit mattem Finish, die selbst einer so profanen Tätigkeit wie dem Lichtanschalten Stil verleihen.

An solchen Details kann man als Bewohner den Unterschied zwischen gut und perfekt ablesen. Und täglich spüren. Um den Firmengründer Peter Heinrich Schmitz zu paraphrasieren: Nur das bleibt erfreulich, was hochwertig ist.

Daniel Miller, professor of anthropology at the renowned University College London, has focused on so-called material culture, i.e. on the question of how a person's personality and living conditions are reflected in the objects with which he surrounds himself within his four walls: from great-grandmother's gold rimmed dinnerware to new, noble Sonus faber loudspeakers or a star chef-worthy stove from Molteni to the scuffed wooden chest of drawers from childhood – comforting, high-quality or memory-laden, but always: emotionally important.

This everyday research on the importance of things in one's own home can also be applied to the home itself: What does an apartment have to be like for us to feel permanently comfortable in it? What makes the house surrounding it a counterpoint to the restless outside? To achieve this, RALF SCHMITZ relies on a selection of proven beauty from other eras, on building elements that have always stood for generosity, elegance and style. The work is carried out by craftsmen who, whether plasterers, stonemasons, locksmiths, parquet layers, window or stair builders, are all true masters of their trade and still versed in the traditional arts.

Solid on the one hand – highly emotional on the other: Because the soft curve of a forged doorknob delights the person who touches it every time. Minimally irregular natural stone tiles in the bathroom not only ground bare feet, they are almost eternally durable and timelessly beautiful. The clack of heels on elegant oak parquet announces the loved one you've been waiting for.

"Stucco is old glamour and traditional craftsmanship, not luxury," Ulrich Jacobi comments. For more than 30 years, the master craftsman and his 20 employees have been working to make historic buildings beautiful again – and new buildings more magnificent. For the SCHMITZ House on Eisenzahnstraße, he supplied more than 1,000 meters of handmade stucco moldings; the specially built templates made of wood and sheet metal included almost 15 different motif shapes developed by architect Sebastian Treese.

The special, aesthetically outstanding continues in the more public areas of each SCHMITZ house: Mailboxes made of patinated brass and strikingly framed in dark wood make even letters from the tax office about the corporate tax return with attachment OG enjoyable (well, almost anyway). In keeping with the exotic flair of the new apartment house Alexander, designer Oliver Jungel opted for Berker switches in a special brass with a matte finish for the stairwells, which lend style even to such a mundane activity as switching on the lights.

Residents can tell the difference between good and perfect from details like these. And feel it every day. To paraphrase company founder Peter Heinrich Schmitz: Only that which is high-quality remains pleasing.

———————

Riesige Bogenfenster,
Kaminmasken und
Klingeln sind oft eigens
gefertigte Unikate

One-of-a-kind: Huge arched windows,
chimney masks and bell plates are often specially crafted

Rasant: Bruno Perla, ein samtdunkler Marmor mit markanter Äderung, rahmt diesen Kamin. Linke Seite: Rund zwei Wochen arbeitete man in der Berliner Kunstschmiede Fittkau an jeder Fenstertür für die Lobby der Eisenzahnstraße; die 3,70 m hohen Unikate wiegen 150 Kilo

Bruno Perla, a veined dark marble, creates a strikingly framed open fire. Left page: Every French lobby door took the Fittkau artisan smithery around two weeks to finish; the altogether three unique pieces are 3.7 m in height and weigh around 150 kilos

Schön und sicher dank diskret integriertem Alarmtransponder; Klingelschild aus Baubronze mit erhabenem Logo und Firmennamen

Style and security: discreetly integrated alarm transponder; bell plate crafted from architectural bronze

BUILDING EXCEPTIONAL HOMES

TEXT **Holger Reiners**   ILLUSTRATIONEN **Sebastian Treese Architekten**

Bewährte Baukunst als Basis: Mit zeitloser Ästhetik trägt
RALF SCHMITZ die Eleganz klassischer Architektur in die Zukunft.

Lasting architecture as a foundation:
With timeless aesthetics, RALF SCHMITZ carries the elegance
of classical architecture into the future.

HAMBURG

CHARLOTTE-NIESE-STRASSE
Sebastian Treese Architekten
4 Stadthäuser und 1 Villa mit
Wohnflächen von 230 bis 350 qm

KARLSTRASSE
Sebastian Treese Architekten
10 Wohnungen von 80 bis 287 qm

ROOSENS WEG
Petra und Paul Kahlfeldt Architekten
5 Wohnungen, darunter
1 Penthouse, von 135 bis 258 qm

KEMPEN

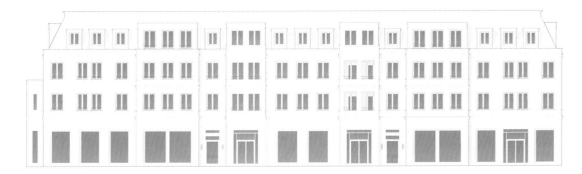

KLOSTERHOF
RKW Architektur +
Wohn- und Geschäftshaus
mit 2500 qm Gewerbefläche
und 39 Apartments

PETERSTRASSE / DONKWALL
Sebastian Treese Architekten
2 Stadtvillen rahmen das barocke
Baudenkmal mit insgesamt
13 Wohnungen von 74 bis 153 qm
und 1 Gewerbefläche

Schönheit und Eleganz. Diese Begriffe sorgen seit Jahren für heftige Diskussionen unter Architekten. Darf man denn heute noch so bauen wie im Stil von vor über 100 Jahren, ist das nicht ein Verrat an der Moralität des Berufsstandes? Würde uns nicht so eine scheinbar heile Welt angeboten, wird Architektur nicht so zum Seelentröster in einem rauen Alltag, obwohl sie doch besser andere Prioritäten setzen sollte? Hardliner unter den heutigen Architekten kämpfen verbissen um die sogenannte Moderne mit ihren Stereotypen und um ihr Entwurfsprinzip des rechten Winkels als Maß aller Dinge.

RALF SCHMITZ hat sich jedoch nie um irgendeinen oktroyierten Mainstream gekümmert. Als Auftraggeber renommierter Entwurfsbüros ist das Unternehmen stets konsequent seiner ganz eigenen Sicht auf Architektur gefolgt, einer Architektur der Eleganz und des Wohlbefindens. Nennen wir es doch – ebenso einfach wie kompliziert – so: Es soll Schönheit entstehen. Dies umzusetzen ist eine Gratwanderung, denn das Staunen über das Phänomen Schönheit und die Versuche, Schönheit zu definieren, zählen seit der Antike, seit Platons Satz, das Schöne sei der Glanz des Wahren *(pulchrum est splendor veri)*, zu den wichtigsten Themen der Philosophie. Schönheit kommt mithin vom Scheinen – nicht im Sinne einer bloßen Vorspiegelung, sondern vom Leuchten, vom Glänzen. Der Glanz der Wahrheit, der Wirklichkeit ist also das Schöne.

Und dies kann eigentlich jeder erkennen. Denn die biologische Forschung hat ergeben, dass wir alle eine Art Kunst- und Symmetrie-Gen in uns tragen, dass wir alle also jene Parameter der Schönheit wahrnehmen, die seit Platon nichts an ihrer Gültigkeit eingebüßt haben. Was ist die Fassade eines Hauses anderes als ein Gesicht – das ist ja der Ursprung des Wortes Fassade. Ein schönes Gesicht, eine einladende Fassade heben unsere Stimmung, sie sind

Beauty and elegance. These terms have long been the subject of heated discussions among architects. Can contemporary architecture still follow the style of centuries past or is that a betrayal of the morality of the profession? If it can thus channel a seemingly ideal world, doesn't architecture deliver a kind of solace for the soul in the harsh reality of quotidian life, even though it could or should be focusing on other priorities? Hardliners among contemporary architects argue stubbornly for so-called modernist architecture with all of its stereotypes and its focus on right angles above everything else.

RALF SCHMITZ, however, has never cared about any imposed mainstream. As a client of renowned design offices, the company has always and consistently followed its very own view of architecture: an architecture of elegance and well-being. Let's put it this way, a concept both simple and complex: the results must be beautiful. This requires a delicate balance, because marveling at beauty and attempting to define beauty have been some of philosophy's most important debates since antiquity, since the statement, oft attributed to Plato, that beauty is the splendor of truth: *pulchrum est splendor veri.* Thus, beauty is to be found in its apparition, not as a mere contrivance, but from its radiance, its brilliance. The glow of truth, of reality, is what is beautiful.

And actually everyone can recognize this. Because biological research has shown that we all carry a kind of art and symmetry gene within us, that humans all perceive those parameters of beauty that have lost none of their validity since Plato. What is the facade of a house but a face – that is, after all, the origin of the word. A beautiful face, an inviting facade lift our mood, they are a perceptual balm for us. All counter-movements of architecture failed with a short expiry date – however, their built results continue to harass our aesthetic perception for decades to come, as unfortunately any walk through any metropolis shows.

DÜSSELDORF

CARMENSTRASSE
Sebastian Treese Architekten
2 Residenzen mit je rund 320 qm

RUBENSSTRASSE
Sebastian Treese Architekten
5 Townhouses mit insgesamt
1335 qm Wohnfläche

ACHENBACHSTRASSE
Sebastian Treese Architekten
18 Wohnungen mit 118 bis 196 qm

HEINSBERGSTRASSE
Sebastian Treese Architekten
4 Wohnungen von 102 bis 195 qm

GERHARD-DOMAGK-STRASSE
RKW Architektur +
20 Wohnungen sowie 2 Maisonette-
Townhouses von 110 bis 300 qm

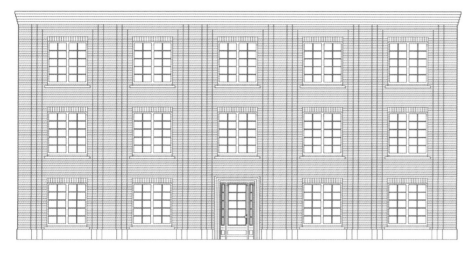

BILKER STRASSE
Kessel und Züger Architekten
Ensemble aus Vorder- und Hofhaus mit
10 Wohnungen von 150 bis 263 qm

GREIFWEG
Sebastian Treese Architekten
3 Gebäude mit 14 Wohnungen und
2 Penthouses von 114 bis 204 qm

RHEINALLEE
Sebastian Treese Architekten
2 Townhouses mit je 360 qm

DEGERSTRASSE
RKW Architektur +
11 Wohnungen von 139 bis 245 qm,
darunter 2 Maisonette-
Townhouses mit Privatgärten im Hof

„Wir glauben, dass ein
neues Gebäude
kein Fremdkörper in seinem
Umfeld sein soll"

Axel Martin Schmitz
"We believe that a new building should not be a foreign
body in its surroundings"

für uns ein Wahrnehmungsbalsam. Alle Gegenbewegungen der Architektur scheiterten mit kurzem Verfallsdatum – jedoch belästigen ihre gebauten Ergebnisse unsere ästhetische Wahrnehmung noch über Jahrzehnte hinaus, wie leider jeder Spaziergang durch eine beliebige Metropole zeigt.

Das Unternehmen RALF SCHMITZ schafft dagegen architektonische Adressen, die nicht nur jeden Bewohner auch ästhetisch glücklich machen, sondern jedem Menschen im öffentlichen Raum visuell zugänglich sind und mit staunender Freude wahrgenommen werden: ein unterschwelliger, freudiger Impuls am Weg.

„Die Fassade eines Hauses, also sein Gesicht, ist keine private Angelegenheit, sondern eine öffentliche"

Ralf Schmitz
"The facade of a house, its face, is not a private matter but a public one"

Die langfristige Verantwortung, einen Beitrag zum Gesicht einer Stadt zu leisten, zu einem gewachsenen Viertel, wird ernst genommen. „Die Fassade eines Hauses, also sein Gesicht, ist keine private Angelegenheit, sondern eine öffentliche", sagt Ralf Schmitz dazu, und sein Sohn Axel Martin ergänzt: „Wir glauben, dass ein neues Gebäude kein Fremdkörper in seinem Umfeld sein soll."

Dies gelingt, weil für die Projektentwürfe in Kempen, Düsseldorf, Berlin, Hamburg und demnächst in Köln nur sorgfältig ausgewählte und sehr renommierte Büros beauftragt werden. Deren Vorstellungen harmonieren aufs Beste mit den hohen Ansprüchen des Traditionsunternehmens, dessen baukulturelle Wurzeln bis ins Jahr 1864 zurückreichen.

Die Stadtvillen und Stadthäuser von RALF SCHMITZ stellen sich in ihrer stolzen und doch zurückhaltenden Würde sowohl dem Betrachter als vor allem auch dem Bewohner als die Botschafter eines eleganten Zuhauses dar. Für die Käufer eines solchen Domizils wird es das Passepartout für die eigene Lebenswelt. Erlesene Materialien, gekonnte Verarbeitung und raffinierte Einbauten, überhaupt die außerordentliche Detaillierung des Gebauten im Äußeren wie auch im Inneren als Gesamtkunstwerk, dienen als reizvolle, zu bespielende Grundlage einer persönlichen Möblierung durch die neuen Eigentümer.

Das ist die große Kunst der Bauwerke aus dem Hause RALF SCHMITZ: Alle Projekte, stets geprägt von der allgegenwärtigen Liebe zur Architektur, bieten ein elegantes Ambiente als Fond für eigene Wohnvorstellungen von Privatheit und Repräsentation. Und zugleich bilden sie in den Straßen und an den Plätzen, an denen sie entstehen, reizvolle architektonische Besonderheiten, weil sie einer zeitlosen Formensprache huldigen.

Schönheit ist eben noch immer der Glanz der Wahrheit.

The RALF SCHMITZ firm, however, creates homes that not only please every inhabitant aesthetically, but are visually accessible and received with delight by every passerby: a subliminally joyful boost along the way. The long-term responsibility to contribute to the face of a city, to an established neighborhood, is taken seriously. "The facade of a building, its face, is not a private matter, but a public one," Ralf Schmitz says in this regard, and his son adds, "We believe that a new building should not be a foreign body in its surroundings."

This succeeds because only carefully selected and very renowned offices are commissioned for the project designs in Kempen, Düsseldorf, Berlin, Hamburg and soon in Cologne. These firms' ideas harmonize perfectly with the high standards of the long-established company, whose architectural roots go back to 1864.

RALF SCHMITZ buildings and townhouses present themselves in proud yet reserved dignity to the beholder, but above all to their inhabitants as shining examples of the archetypal elegant domicile. For the buyers of such homes, they become the framework for their particular style of living. Exquisite materials, skillful workmanship and ingenious built-ins – in fact, all of the extraordinary detail of the building both inside and out, as a complete work of art – serve as a delightful basis for the new owners to furnish and decorate to their personal taste.

This is the great achievement of all the construction projects: These creations, always shaped by the ever-present love of architecture, offer an elegant ambience as the setting for one's own ideas of how to live in both public and private spheres. And at the same time, they form charming architectural features on the streets and squares where they are built, because they pay homage to a timeless formal language.

Beauty is, after all, still the splendor of truth.

SIGMARINGER STRASSE
Sebastian Treese Architekten
12 Wohnungen von 64 bis 184 qm

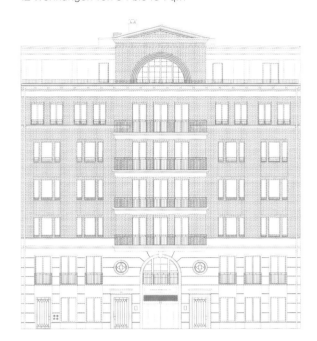

PREUSSENALLEE
Sebastian Treese Architekten
4 Einheiten von 132 bis 180 qm

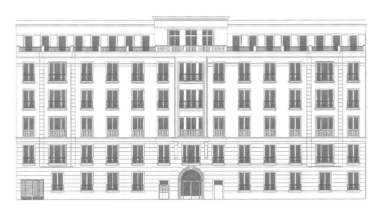

EISENZAHNSTRASSE
Sebastian Treese Architekten
Stadtpalais beim Kurfürstendamm
mit 12 Domizilen von 192 bis 467 qm
in Kooperation mit Bottega Veneta

EMSER STRASSE
Sebastian Treese Architekten
Leuchtturmprojekt mit Privatpark,
42 Einheiten von 50 bis 650 qm

BERLIN

LINIENSTRASSE
Sebastian Treese Architekten
7 Wohnungen, darunter 1 Penthouse,
von 93 bis 212 qm

WERNERSTRASSE
Petra und Paul Kahlfeldt Architekten
2 Stadtvillen mit je 3 Wohnungen
von 211 bis 308 qm

Brit Chic in Düsseldorfs Zooviertel:
Markante Erker akzentuieren die
langlebige charmante Klinkerfassade.

Brit Chic in Düsseldorf's Zoo district:
Striking bay windows accentuate
the long-lasting charming brick facade.

DRESSED
IN RED

TEXT **Bettina Schneuer** FOTOS **Noshe, Christian Stoll**

ACHENBACHSTRASSE,
DÜSSELDORF ZOO

Klinker aus einer Traditionsmanu-
faktur, bei 1200 Grad gebrannt
und ohne chemische Zusätze,
umhüllen die Fassade – Bögen
und Erker geben ihr Rhythmus

Clinker bricks from a traditional
manufactory, fired at 1,200 degrees
Celsius and without chemical
additives, envelop the facade, arches
and bay windows give it rhythm

„Großbürgerlich wohnen bedeutet heute: großzügig und gelassen"

Sebastian Treese, Architekt
"Urban patrician living today means: generous and serene"

Exklusivität in den schönsten Vierteln: Seit Jahrzehnten schon baut RALF SCHMITZ von der Carlstadt bis Oberkassel in den Bestlagen Düsseldorfs beidseits des Rheins. Dieser Anspruch verpflichtet – gegenüber denen, die hinter diesen eleganten Fassaden leben, wie auch gegenüber jenen, die an den zeitlos-schönen Gebäuden vorbeigehen.

Und so ist das Unternehmen besonders stolz auf das Haus Achenbach 43 im begehrten Zooviertel, das erneut beide Ziele vereint. Malerische Vorgärten liegen vor der schmucken Fassade, aus der im gleichmäßigen Rhythmus Erker hervorspringen. Dieses markante Relief strukturiert die 45 Meter lange Backsteinfront, der Rundbögen und Gesimsbänder zusätzlich Klasse verleihen. Aus den Erkerräumen, die als Küche, Homeoffice oder offene Loggia fungieren, öffnet sich aus gleich drei bodentiefen Fenstern oder Öffnungen der Blick die Straße hinauf und hinab – und als Bewohner fühlt man sich, als säße man in den Kronen der ehrwürdigen Platanen. Auch die Garagenzufahrt mit klassischem Holztor und die beiden aufwendig gestalteten Hauseingänge hinter dem „roten Teppich", der Zuwegung aus Backsteinpflaster, betonen die ästhetische Symmetrie.

Der verwendete Wittmunder Klinker aus der gleichnamigen ostfriesischen Manufaktur, bei 1200 Grad gebrannt und ohne chemische Zusätze, umhüllt das Haus wie ein Kleid in warmem Ziegelrot – die Wand als Gewand. Eine Vielzahl von Sonderformaten für die Bögen untermauert im Wortsinne den handwerklichen Anspruch, für den die Familie Schmitz seit nunmehr 160 Jahren steht. Dauerhaft, hochwertig und dennoch anmutig – dieses Premiumprojekt reiht sich ein in die klassische Düsseldorfer Backsteinbaukultur.

In den hohen Entrees beginnt eine andere Welt: Wie britische Herrenhäuser empfangen die Eingangshallen mit klassischen Wandtäfelungen, Dielenböden, Zierprofilen an den Decken und warmem Licht. Via zwei Aufzüge oder über die ansehnlichen Treppenhäuser erreicht man die insgesamt 18 Wohnungen mit Flächen von 118 bis 196 Quadratmetern plus Außenbereichen; die beiden größten Attika-Einheiten ganz oben bieten beidseitig Terrassen. Pro Haus gibt es auf jeder Etage nur zwei Einheiten, die sich von der Straße bis zum rückwärtigen Gartenhof erstrecken und daher ausgezeichnet belichtet werden; dazu kommt die stattliche Raumhöhe von bis zu drei Metern. Kluge Grundrisse machen Flure fast überflüssig: Raumfluchten und Flügeltüren mit Glaseinsätzen vermitteln herrschaftliche Großzügigkeit. Das Flair eines Altbaus ergänzt moderner Komfort: Zu den schicken Briefkastenanlagen aus patiniertem Messing gehören praktische Paketstationen, die Tiefgarage bietet 21 Stellplätze, die teils vorgerüstet sind für Elektromobilität; dazu kommen Räume für Räder und Kinderwägen.

Exclusivity in the most beautiful neighborhoods: For decades, RALF SCHMITZ has been building in Düsseldorf's prime locations on both sides of the Rhine, from Carlstadt to Oberkassel. This privilege obliges – on the one hand towards those who live behind these elegant facades, on the other hand towards those who pass by the timelessly beautiful buildings.

And so the company is particularly proud of Achenbach 43 in the coveted Zoo district, which once again combines both goals. Picturesque gardens lie in front of the neat facade, from which oriel windows jut out in a regular rhythm. This striking relief structures the 45-meter-long brick facade, to which round arches and cornice bands lend additional class. From the orieled rooms, which function as kitchens, home offices or open loggias, the view up and down the street opens out of no less than three floor-to-ceiling windows or openings – and as a resident, you feel as if you are sitting in the crowns of the venerable plane trees. The garage entrance with its classic wooden gate and the two elaborately designed building entrances behind the "red carpet," the brick paved access, also emphasize the aesthetic symmetry.

The Wittmund clinker used, from the homonymous East Frisian manufactory, fired at 1,200 degrees Celsius and without chemical additives, envelops the house like a dress in warm brick red – the wall as a garment. A variety of special formats for the arches underpin the craftsmanship for which the RALF SCHMITZ company has stood for 160 years. Durable, high-quality, yet graceful – this premium project joins the venerable club of classic Düsseldorf brick buildings.

A different world begins in the high entrance halls: like stately British homes, the foyers beckon with classic wall paneling, plank floors, decorative moldings on the ceilings and warm light. The 18 apartments with floor areas ranging from 118 to 196 square meters plus outdoor areas are accessed via two elevators or the impressive staircases; the two largest top-floor units offer terraces on both sides. There are only two units per house on each floor, which extend from the street to the rear garden courtyard and are therefore excellently lit; in addition, there is the impressive room height of up to three meters. Clever floor plans make corridors almost superfluous: Double doors with glass inserts connecting the enfilade convey a sense of grandeur.

The flair of an old building is complemented by modern comfort: chic mailboxes made of patinated brass include practical parcel stations, a garage offers 21 parking spaces, some of which are pre-equipped for electric mobility; there are also rooms for bicycles and strollers.

Rückwärtig liegen vier Gärten
im Sondernutzungsrecht; die zwei
größten Attika-Einheiten bieten
beidseitig große Dachterrassen.
Linke Seite: Die Garage mit edlem
Holztor umfasst 21 Stellplätze

Four gardens with special rights of
use are in the rear; the garage with a
majestic doorway contains 21 parking
spaces. The two largest top-floor
units offer roof terraces on both sides

„Architektur beginnt,
wenn zwei Backsteine sorgfältig
zusammengesetzt werden"

Ludwig Mies van der Rohe
"Architecture begins when two bricks are carefully put together"

Bauen aus Leidenschaft:
Einem Versprechen verpflichtet

KEMPEN, HERBST 2022

Dr. Axel Martin Schmitz

Vertreter der fünften Generation:
Axel Martin Schmitz stieg 2011 in das
Familienunternehmen ein, seit 2013
ist der promovierte Betriebswirt
geschäftsführender Gesellschafter

Vor über elf Jahren bin ich in das Familienunternehmen eingetreten. Im Rückblick war es der Wunsch, etwas von Dauer zu schaffen, etwas, das nachhaltig ist und Menschen bewegt. Damit meine ich nicht nur die Bewohner, sondern jeden, der das Haus erleben kann, ob als Besucher oder Passant. Etwas, das mir im vorherigen Beruf nicht vergönnt war und ich als großes Privileg betrachte. Jedem Haus eine eigene Seele mitzugeben, kostet Kraft und Herzblut und ich behaupte bis heute, schon anhand einer ersten Visualisierung sehen zu können, ob schon genug davon drinsteckt. Umso mehr Bewunderung habe ich für meinen Vater entwickelt, der bereits 45 Jahre unermüdlich mit diesem Anspruch im Unternehmen wirkt und schon so viel Herzblut aufgewendet haben muss. Es ist daher mehr als wohlverdient, wenn er sich jetzt nach dem Abschluss seines Leuchtturmprojekts Alexander (S. 8 ff.) mehr der Familie widmen möchte – dem Unternehmen wird er aber weiterhin mit Rat und Tat zur Seite stehen, wofür ich unendlich dankbar bin.

Der zweite Band unserer Reihe EXCEPTIONAL HOMES ist vollendet: Mit großer Freude und auch Stolz blicken wir mit Ihnen auf diese beeindruckende Werkschau der letzten Jahre. Denn seit 2017, seit der Veröffentlichung des ersten Bandes, hat sich viel Neues getan. Mit unserem neuesten Projekt in der Villenkolonie Marienburg erschließen wir nun die Kulturhauptstadt Köln. Auch an unseren bewährten Standorten von Düsseldorf bis Berlin entstanden und entstehen weiter wegweisende Gebäude, bleiben wir weiter auf der Suche nach Raum für das Außergewöhnliche.

Glücklich bin ich, dass wir in den letzten Jahren zunehmend Menschen für unsere Idee begeistern konnten, Kunden, die dies alles erst ermöglichen, die unsere Ansicht teilen, das bewährt Gute zu erhalten und es noch besser zu machen. Menschen, die einen besonderen Ort suchen, an dem sie sich wohlfühlen, ohne etwas zur Schau zu tragen. Kunden, welche es richtig finden, in einem Haus zu wohnen, das sich in seine Umgebung einfügt, solche, die Baukultur erkennen und zu bewahren bereit sind. Denn das Zeitlose lädt uns ein, es umhüllt uns, es bietet über Generationen Geborgenheit.

Die damit verbundene Verantwortung fühle ich bei Spaziergängen durch Kempen, Düsseldorf, Berlin und Hamburg – durch die Städte, deren Gesichter mitzugestalten unser Glück und unsere Chance ist. Das ist die Leidenschaft und Berufung, der wir auch weiterhin folgen werden: neue Herausforderungen zu meistern, zukunftsweisend zu sein in unserer besonderen Verbindung von Zeitlosigkeit und modernem Komfort. Meine Zuversicht, dass uns dieses Versprechen auch in Zukunft zu erfüllen gelingt, schöpfe ich aus der Begegnung mit den Menschen, die jeden Tag mit mir an diesem Ziel arbeiten, und denen, die es lieben, in diesen Häusern zu leben – oder sich einfach an einem Buch wie diesem hier erfreuen können.

I joined the family firm over 11 years ago. In retrospect, what motivated me was the desire to create something for the ages, something that was sustainable and that moved people. Not just the inhabitants, but anyone who experienced the home, either as visitors or passersby. This is something I consider a huge privilege, something not granted to me in my previous career. Imbuing each building with its own soul requires energy and lifeblood, and I believe that I can recognize, from the first visualization, if enough of either element is present in any given project. Over time, I have developed even more admiration for my father who has, for the past 45 years, worked tirelessly with this standard as his guiding light, investing so much lifeblood along the way. Now that his flagship development The Alexander (p. 8 ff) has been completed, he has more than earned the right to spend more time with his family – but he continues to support the firm with his guidance and advice, for which I am endlessly grateful.

The second volume of our series EXCEPTIONAL HOMES is complete: We take great pleasure and pride in looking back on this impressive exhibition of our projects over the past few years. A lot has happened since 2017, when the first volume was published. With our newest development in the residential villa neighborhood of Marienburg, we have now tapped into Cologne, a European capital of culture. But we also remain ever on the lookout for extraordinary spaces for our groundbreaking buildings in the cities we've long developed in, like Düsseldorf and Berlin.

I'm pleased that in recent years we've been able to attract increasing numbers of people to our ideas; customers who have made this all possible and who share our point of view, to preserve that which we know is good and to constantly strive to improve it. People who seek out special locations where they feel at home without having to show off. Customers who like to live in homes that fit perfectly into the surrounding neighborhood, who recognize good building culture and are prepared to uphold it. The timeless invites us in, envelops us and offers a feeling of comfort that lasts for generations.

I feel the responsibility that comes therewith on strolls through Kempen, Düsseldorf, Berlin and Hamburg – through the cities whose portraits we've had the good fortune and opportunity to help shape. It is this passion and this calling that we will continue to follow: to master new challenges and to face the future with our unique combination of timelessness and modern comforts. The confidence I have in our potential to fulfill these promises in the future stems from the encounters I have with those who work on these goals daily, as well as those who love to live in these homes – or who find joy leafing through the pages of a book like this one.

CREDITS

IMPRINT

Herausgeber / Publisher: RALF SCHMITZ GmbH
Konzept / Concept: Bettina Schneuer, André M. Wyst
Art Direktor / Art Direction: André M. Wyst
Chefredaktion / Editor-in-Chief: Bettina Schneuer
Text / Texts: Rainer Haubrich, Ina Marie Kühnast, Tanja Pabelick,
Holger Reiners, Iris Rodriguez, Nora Scharer, Axel Martin Schmitz, Bettina Schneuer,
Florian Siebeck, Sebastian Treese, Christian Tröster

Lektorat / Copyediting: Claudia Kühne, Luisa Weiss
Übersetzung / Translation: Luisa Weiss
Projektmanagement / Project Management: Friederike von Greve, Nora Scharer
Beratung / Consulting: Nadine Barth
Verlagskoordination / Coordination: Sonja Altmeppen

Schrift / Typeface: Suisse Int'l, Adobe Caslon Pro
Verlagsherstellung / Production: Thomas Lemaître, Hatje Cantz
Papier / Paper: GardaMatt Art, 170 g/m^2
Druck und Bindung / Printing and Binding: Printer Trento

Erschienen im / Published by:
Hatje Cantz Verlag GmbH
Mommsenstraße 27
10629 Berlin
Deutschland / Germany
www.hatjecantz.com
Ein Unternehmen der Ganske Verlagsgruppe /
A Ganske Publishing Group Company

ISBN: 978-3-7757-5389-0
Printed in Italy

Umschlagabbildung / Cover illustration: Sebastian Treese Architekten
Frontispiz / Frontispiece: Arbeiter auf einer Baustelle der Heinrich Schmitz KG

EXCEPTIONAL
HOMES
SINCE 1864

The Classic Style of RALF SCHMITZ

RALF SCHMITZ GmbH
Moorenring 29, 47906 Kempen
Tel 02152 9177-0
mail@ralfschmitz.com

RALFSCHMITZ.COM

RS

Ralf Schmitz und *Dr. Axel Martin Schmitz*
im September 2022 vor der
Achenbachstraße 43 in Düsseldorf